Also by Norman K. Whitcomb:

The Whitcomb Family History, February 2008
Gateway Press. 534 pp, *illustrated and indexed.*
The History of the family from 1249.

Available directly from the author at: Whitcombs2@aol.com

MYOPIC MAN

by

Norman K. Whitcomb
Denver, Colorado

iUniverse, Inc.
New York   Bloomington

Myopic Man
Can a united church prevent the collapse of the American Empire?

Copyright © 2010 Myopic Man

iUniverse books may be ordered through booksellers or by contacting:

iUniverse
1663 Liberty Drive
Bloomington, IN 47403
www.iuniverse.com
1-800-Authors (1-800-288-4677)

ISBN: 978-1-4502-2622-6 (pbk)
ISBN: 978-1-4502-2624-0 (cloth)
ISBN: 978-1-4502-2623-3 (ebk)

Library of Congress Control Number: 2010905427

Printed in the United States of America

iUniverse rev. date: 4/30/2010

For my cellist wife Marcia

who lovingly reviewed the text

and made very helpful comments

CONTENTS

LIST OF FIGURES & TABLES

PREFACE

I believe the American Empire is in danger of collapse much like the Roman Empire fifteen centuries ago. Our government is enroute to being one *"of the corporation, by the corporation, and for the corporation."* I believe a united church is the only vehicle that can voice ethical reform in our nation to prevent its collapse, both financially and ethically. I devote the last three chapters to this topic.

I feel it is important for all of us to understand what constrains our thinking. Therefore, in Chapter One I describe those factors, which I believe blinds us today, and similarly limited the worldview of the Biblical writers millennia ago. To me, the Bible is not a science textbook, but an expression of people's experience of God written in the metaphorical language of their time.

In order to unite the church, individuals must know what they believe so that they can unite around a common creed and purpose. I take you through a good deal of church history so you can understand how the church beliefs evolved. I take you through the main questions of faith as I looked at them, so that you may take a similar journey. For the non-religious this material is a condensed exposition of Christian beliefs that should wipe away the mysteries of the church.

I see the disintegration of Protestant denominations, and the birth of an American Catholic church that will be part of the united church. The death of denominations should not be fought, but rather the unification of the church should be sought.

The book is forward-looking and hopefully, will give you reason to see what is necessary to save our nation. I have written for inquisitive and socially motivated persons, both religious and non-religious, that have an interest in seeing a reformed society. Clergy of both Protestant and reformed Catholic backgrounds will find the discussion on unity enticing.

CHAPTER 1

MYOPIA

A blind man knows he is blind, but those who see may not know that they also are blind. We are like birds in a cage, constrained by many things we may or may not see. We must understand that which constrains us so we will not stumble.

Introduction

I see an America that is in trouble. It is led by special interests that have caused economic injustice in our society. Further, there are misplaced priorities in our culture. I describe the problems in Chapter Nine, and compare the factors that led to the collapse of the Roman Empire with the symptoms prevalent in the American Empire that could lead to its collapse. We must take some corrective actions to prevent America from collapsing in upon itself. I fail to see that either Wall Street or Washington will prevent the collapse since they are part of the source of our problems. I believe only a unified Christian church working with other religious and social bodies that will stand together for economic justice and social reordering of American priorities can save us.

The Romans probably didn't expect their Empire to collapse. Few of us in America see our own possible collapse. Individual economists and scholars see today that the vast inequality of national wealth is doing more harm than good. The church must unite and stand for social justice and reordered national priorities that we can all own and be proud of. This book is about a journey to achieve that goal.

The church of today must move from self-preservation to passion, and from legalism to love. It is hopelessly divided and weak. It does not have a voice that can be heard. It competes with itself, and is self-protective. Secular groups are leading the way for social reform. Where is that church of the first century that went out into the world to reform it and change its priorities? Why is the church of today a follower and not a leader?

Karen Armstrong, the noted Catholic scholar and expert on Judaism, Islam, and Christianity, suggests that all religions are based on care and compassion, but that we are all groping our way along the same path. It is time that we move from groping to walking boldly.

To become united, we must take a four thousand year journey from early religion, ending some ten to twenty-five years from now in the mid-21st century. By then or sooner we must have a reunified church that can awaken America to its destiny to be a people speaking for the good of all people. America must give up special interests for the common good. The recent Supreme Court decision giving corporations a huge advantage over individual Americans in unlimited political campaign spending must be countered by a unified church that can speak with the strength of 40 million people or more. It must speak for truth, not rhetoric. Our nation must recapture the principle that it should be led by a government of the people, by the people, and for the people.

By 2050, I believe there can be a reunion of the progressive mainline Protestant churches and a new American Catholic Church, which will have separated from Rome. This union could form The Progressive Christian Church of America. The names "Protestant" and "Catholic" should disappear and be replaced with the term "Christian." The Reformation is long over. There needs to be a new marriage of churches. Each can hold to its traditions and particular beliefs, but they should be bonded by the common beliefs that existed when the church was first formed in 325 C.E.

I urge unification not to gain power, but to promote vision. The church must be a voice for the Christ who came to give us a new kingdom. The church in the first Millennium sought power. The church in the second Millennium must seek vision. The idolatry of power and wealth is the work of the Evil One. The tactic of the Evil One is to cloud our vision and deceive us. The work of saving the world from greed must come from God through the church.

Reunifying a church that has been fractured for five hundred years may seem impossible, but it is doable. Leaders must unite around core beliefs and set aside dogma that has divided us. I believe that American laypeople, for the most part, do not particularly understand or own for themselves the divisive dogma that has separated us. Because of this, I lay out in several chapters, a historical journey from the religion of the early Mayans through the evolution of the Hebrew and Christian canons to the point of unification of the Christian church in 325 C.E. in Nicea, Turkey. At this point we will have seen what the unified Christian Church believed. Some centuries after Nicea we will see that the church gained power, abused it, looked upon itself as important and infallible, and created further dogma that led to the division of the church. After reading eight chapters I ask that you decide for yourself what is important to you. I ask that you not repeat those tenets that were taught in your youth, but rather that you think through the questions of faith as an adult and reach your own conclusions, as if you were a theologian. We cannot unify unless we know what we believe and why we believe it.

So we might find those tenets that are essential to church unification, I will share my personal journey through the major questions of faith in Chapter Eight and share with you, as a layperson, my own beliefs..

Before we plunge into religious history and the questions of faith it is important to understand some of the constraints we, and the biblical writers before us, are faced with that cloud our vision. *MYOPIC MAN* is my attempt to give readers an understanding of those factors that have made mankind shortsighted (myopic) and have blinded him in writing and interpreting the scriptures. Look now at how mankind is blinded.

Constraints that blur our Vision

Mankind can see with his eyes and yet be blinded in his mind partially because of his limited worldview and partially because the Evil One does not wish him to see reality. If we don't acknowledge that constraints hinder our vision, then we will be blind. I believe the church of the Middle Ages was blinded by constraints it did not see nor acknowledge, and as a result, made some poor policy decisions.

If there will be a test after this life prior to admittance into the new kingdom, I suspect many of us would flunk. I see so many disparate expressions of religion in our worldwide culture today, I wonder who has it right and who has it wrong. Conservatives, whether Jewish, Christian or Islamic, tend to take their scriptures literally and tout the miraculous powers of God. Some adhere strictly to the many ritual laws found in the Torah. Islamics would follow the directives of Muhammad in the Koran, but possibly misinterpret what Muhammad was trying to say. Some take the scriptures selectively, justifying murder of innocents, while neglecting the pronouncements to honor all people who may follow different religions.

Mankind in a Cage

Picture a bird in a cage. The cage is made of thin wire strands that form a barrier to the bird's escape. The floor of the cage is solid, collecting the inevitable droppings the bird makes. The bird is confined, but protected from the cat. The bird's environment is the living room, or wherever the cage is placed. It sees not the oceans, nor the mountains, just the living room and those who enter it. The bird has a limited view of life.

Today we human beings are also constrained as if in a cage, as were the scriptural writers of old. Our cage is not made of wire strands, but of many unseen barriers. We are bound by our view of life, concept of time, perspective, language, culture, tribalism, imagery, education, or lack thereof, tradition, and the environment in which we exist, to name a few. Man is wrapped up by the bounds that confine him, not comprehending God as He asks us to understand Him, and his actions give witness to his myopia. Let me explain.

Christians follow the examples of Jesus and his disciples. Whatever our belief system, there is one God who has created the universe and all who dwell therein. We may call our Creator God by various names, but He is our spiritual parent. He gives us the freedom of choice to accept and love Him, or to ignore or reject Him. He has given us total freedom in our relationship with Him. With this freedom has also come the responsibility to act as He has invited us.

As a layperson I wonder why there are so many different religions and so many different sets of viewpoints. Why are there so many different interpretations of scripture or differences in the tenets of the church? I find that the many beliefs that religious scholars or church organizations have taken, right or wrong, are of little consequence to me. They are not the essential core beliefs that drive my behavior. A unified church would hold itself together by sharing significant core beliefs and would not spend energy dealing with speculative dogma. There will always be cultural traditions and differences between churches, but its one common bond will be based on our understanding of what God has done to save our wretched band on earth. Only incomprehensible interpretations of scripture will divide us.

The Language of Scripture

The first hurdle we cross is understanding whether God dictated scripture to its writers and whether, in fact, everything written is factually exact and true. The first prime tenet of the Christian church is that the Bible is the single, authoritative exposition of God. It is the foundation upon which we base our religious belief system. We must understand that ordinary people who were inspired by the Spirit wrote the scriptures in response to the impact God had upon them. They expressed themselves as they new how, and in a way that their contemporaries would understand.

Mark, Matthew, and Luke all describe the confession of Peter to Jesus differently (see Mk 8:29, Mt 16:13-23), Lk 9:18-22). Jesus asked the disciples, "Whom do men say that I am?" Peter was the one who said, "You are the Christ (the Messiah)." Mark and Luke stopped there. Only Matthew went on to say that the confession of Peter would be the rock upon which His church would be built. The Roman church interprets Jesus' saying to indicate that Peter was indeed that rock, not the confession, upon which the church would be founded. Because Jesus referred to Peter as *Petros* (a rock), he may have meant that either or both interpretations were true. What we read is that Jesus was talking in metaphoric language using the simile "rock" to mean Peter and/or Peter's confession. The larger picture was that Jesus was the Messiah, the gift and Son of God.

As I have thought about writing this book and codifying my own conception of an incomprehensible and unknowable God, I can only express myself in metaphorical concepts. I cannot say "God is...." I can say only "God is like...." God is of a spiritual dimension, I am of a physical dimension, and I am constrained by my own limited experience of life. The biblical writers were also constrained, so it is understandable they would write metaphorically. The gospel writers wrote for different audiences and emphasized different points to win their audience.

What we must grasp in the conversation between Jesus and Peter is that Peter was the first to understand who Jesus was. He was the Messiah, the holy Son of God. That understanding was much more important to Jesus than who Peter was. The early Roman church had established a hierarchy headed by a pope. To justify the authority of the pope, the church had a built-in bias to interpret Jesus' statement to Peter as the basis that Peter, not the confession of who Jesus was, would be the foundation of the church. This is an example of a constraint. The early church had a bias that it used to its advantage.

Those of us who grew up in Sunday Schools were taught the Bible stories as factual acts of God. These included the burning bush, the writing of the Ten Commandments on the two tablets, the parting of the Red Sea, and all of the miracles that Jesus performed. Even as a young boy I had difficulty accepting stories such as Jonah being swallowed by the whale and living to tell about it.

Most religious scholars indicate that the early Biblical writers wrote these stories as metaphors pointing not to historical facts, but to deeper spiritual meanings. As a retired engineer, I can be comfortable with the position of these stories and miracles as being metaphorical. This position is compatible with science as I know it, and I can be free to look at the deeper spiritual meanings the stories were intended to portray, rather than to stop at their face value.

It may be comforting to take the Biblical stories literally, but we must do the work to understand the deeper meanings the writers wished to express. Through the evolution of religion, clergy and scholars have given an authoritative position to the scriptures. To honor this authority, many have translated the scripture literally, and have cast an inflexible viewpoint on its text. Those of us of western mentality are faced with great contradictions when treating every line of scripture as scientific fact, rather than treating the many obvious contradictions as pictures that give a message of awe and wonder rather than science. It is not sacrilegious to acknowledge that science has given us reasonably accurate depictions of the earth's evolution even if they contradict the creation myths that are common to many different religions.

Scholars, both theologians and historians, have come to understand more nearly, the probable life of Jesus and the early evolution of the Christian church. What shall the church of today do with the historical Jesus? Shall we sing the carol, "O Little Town of Nazareth" instead of " Bethlehem" as one of our Christmas favorites? I suspect that the accuracy of the birthplace is less important than carrying on the tradition. This leads us to ask the question, "What is important in our faith?" What tenets and traditions shall the church retain, and which should it change to acknowledge new information?
I must try to understand the various questions of faith and how and why the evolving church took certain religious positions in its early years. Do these positions make sense in our culture today? I encourage you to make your own examination of religious positions and see if they make sense to you. I will also go on to propose how the church might unify itself and be a stronger rock in a crumbling society.

Male-Dominated Language

Since the beginning of time, the female of almost all species bore the young, nurtured, protected, and fed them. The human male took the role as hunter-provider, then farmer, then tradesman, and finally executive. The male protected his harem and the strongest of the species went on to mate and perpetuate the line. This is to say, that we have grown up in a male-dominated life.

It is natural, then, that the Scriptures of all religions were written primarily by men, for men, and about men. Even God is referred to as "He." The Scriptures; however, say that *God is a Spirit, and they that worship Him, must worship in Spirit and Truth."* God does not have genitalia, He is a Spirit. He may have the mental characteristics of strength of a male, but He also has the love and care of a female. Our language fails us, because we do not have a set of pronouns that can describe a being as both male and female in character.

The Islamic word for God is "Allah." This word means the One True God. It has no plural and has no gender. The Muslims have it right, at least to that point. God to them is a Spirit, neither male nor female, assuming Muhammad may have thought of Allah that way. "God" also has no gender or plural, but we automatically apply a masculine connotation to the word "God", partly because of our cultural bias, and also because Jesus referred to him as "The Father."

I believe that when we die and pass on to a spiritual life we will not have genitalia, we will be personalities. We will neither be white, nor black, nor red or yellow. We will likewise, not be Arabian, or Russian, or American or Japanese. We will be part of a new universal family and will understand life from a totally different perspective than at present.

The church universal has taken the male-bias imprint within the Scriptures as a God-ordained permanent directive that men should have the roles of power and authority, and that women should be the subjects of men. Women were to serve men and men were to serve God. This bias has eroded slowly in the secular world, but the church has been reluctant to allow women into ecclesiastical circles, except within progressive churches. Why is it that the church seems to follow society, but not lead it?

Wake up, religion, Wake up, you leaders Don't point to your various scriptures as license to exclude women and keep them in subservient roles in the church and society. It is time that the Roman Catholic Church ordain women priests. Are they less intelligent or faithful than men? Citing scriptures written from a patriarchal bias is not a reason today to continue this exclusion. Archaic traditions are no reason we should continue to travel with horse and buggy. We will never get anywhere with this mentality.

The myth that Eve was made from Adam's rib is cute, but utterly ridiculous. To use this myth as a basis for the subjugation of women is fallacious and myopic. Other religions may have similar myths in their writings relating to women. Jesus referred to God as the "Father," but He too grew up in the patriarchal society of His time.

God has given us maleness and femaleness as a gift, to share with Him the continuing process of creation. I suspect this may not be relevant in the next life. We should think of ourselves as spiritual beings, and not use maleness as a right to superiority. I doubt that God would develop a society and church based on gender superiority, but rather role responsibility.

Paul may have said, "Wives be subject to your husbands," but we should not take this out of the context in which this verse was written. Paul was a Pharisaic Jew with a cultural mindset that women were inferior to men. Men and women should look upon each other as equals. Applying first-century wisdom to today may not at all be appropriate. Any religion that blindly applies first-century customs to twenty-first century society is misguided. We are all equal in the sight of God, men and women together. God is a Spirit, and we must see Him as a Spirit, not as a masculine hero. Our language betrays us, and we don't challenge its constraints.

Unfortunately, as in today's political culture, change is much less likely to come from above where men are entrenched in power and authority. It is much more likely to come from below among the laity and common people. Let the changes begin. Leaders in power only change things when they are forced to, or when it is politically expedient for them to do so. Rebellions start at the bottom with the oppressed. Civil rights, health-care reform, and same sex-marriages are typical of movements that have started at the bottom. Church and social reform will likewise come from the bottom.

Language Must Express Truth

Society depends on accurate language, and words that give clear meaning. Governments, above all, must not be allowed to get away with twisting reality, by misusing language for political purposes. Edwin Newman, the late journalist of a few decades ago, was a champion of the accurate use of language. His message is ever more important today. I believe it is important for the media to use clear language in reporting to the people. It is important for the people to demand clear language from its leaders. It is further important, that religious leaders avoid religious clichés and euphemistic language. Society will only survive if it uses and knows truth.

When people or institutions wish to distort reality, they will use language that is exaggerated and biased. Extremists, whether political or religious, now seem to use deceptive rhetoric to promote their views. The extremist (individual or group) sees his opponent as an enemy and hates that enemy for who he is or what he does. The extremist sees himself, or society, as the victim of the enemy. The extremist thereby elevates himself to the hero who must conquer the enemy. First, the language describing the enemy is exaggerated and the facts are further obfuscated.

The Evil One distorts truth and one's view of it. Suicide bombers have been deluded to believe they are doing God's will and will be rewarded with a place in Paradise for their actions. They fail to see this mindset as evil. Religion cannot be the ally of the Evil One by escalating language and hatred for purposes that are unjust. We must respect each other.

Our World View

We sit on a small planet in a little solar system in the obscure Milky Way Galaxy. Our ancestors may have been able to see 50 miles or so. They saw the sun and the moon, and the faint stars at night. They had absolutely no concept of the immensity of the creation that God had spun off into limitless space. The forefathers knew only what they saw. The bird in the cage had no concept of mountains or ocean. The living room was its universe.

Moses knew a captive and perhaps cantankerous people who desperately wanted freedom. He knew about escaping Pharaoh's chariots, and knew about leading a wandering nation in the desert for a generation. The Torah was written with this worldview.

The bankers of Wall Street have high-rise office buildings as a worldview. They see primarily their own social strata. They don't see derelict houses in Detroit or other Michigan cities. They don't see the empty kitchen tables of the unemployed or the widow who tries to live on a Social Security check of $800/month. Their worldview is narrow, like it is for most of us. It is time for each of us to expand our worldview beyond our local environment.

Time And Creation

Consider time as one of the bounds that constrained the Biblical writers. We live on a planet that rotates about an axis making a complete rotation in what we have defined as one day or 24 hours. Who among us does not wear a watch to guide us through this 24-hour period? We think in terms of hours, days or perhaps months.

I wrote the short story that follows during the summer of 2007 while taking a course at Ghost Ranch, New Mexico.

> A man died and arrived in Heaven and immediately felt the presence of God. He said, "God, may I ask you a few questions?" God said, *"Yes my son, I'll try to answer them."* He said, "The Bible says you created the world and the universe in six days." God said, *"That's what they wrote about me."*
>
> "Well, what took you so long; you could have created the universe in a second by the mere thought of it?" God said, *"I did."* But, the man argued, "Scientists say it took 13 billion years for the universe to form since the Big Bang." God said, *"That is a second, my son."* I asked, "What did you do before the Big Bang?" God said, *"I had an earlier universe during which I created the angels."*

God does not sit on a planet or star that revolves about an axis in a specific time period. He is not constrained by time the way we are. We must understand God in a totally different dimension than we experience on earth. Days and millennia are meaningless to God because He lives in a timeless environment. When we pass from this life, we also shall move into a timeless existence. There is no need to have your watch buried with you. Neither is there a need to hold on to a literal interpretation of the biblical myth about creation. To hold to a six-day creation period as opposed to thirteen billion years is a meaningless distortion of God's act

The biblical writers knew what a day was, but they had no concept of a billion years. They had no concept of an expanding universe, nor that light has a speed. They expressed themselves as they knew life. The point of the creation story is that God created the universe and He proclaimed it good. The time it took is immaterial.

In truth, we are in the first minute of the first day of creation right now. Stars are being formed and elements are being created. God has given us the indescribable gift of being able to create human life on our own, as he breathes the spirit of life into the children we create. This gift He gives jointly and equally to men and women. He endows us with the spirit to nurture and care for our young and to teach them the skills to survive and thrive in society.

Creation, to the myopic, is a past, completed event; to the enlightened, it is a current, and on-going event.

Perspective

The myopic, as a rule, determine truth from a single point of view. Few questions are asked and alternative viewpoints are eschewed. Unfortunately this especially applies to religion as a whole. Many Christians, Jews, Muslims and those of other faiths are myopic when it comes to looking at things objectively. If we can look far-sightedly we may find the mode upon which faith traditions can walk together. The far-sighted approach uses the words of faith as springboards to a larger picture.

Consider the following story that evolved out of the early Christian church. I will use a mythical Pope as the main character, even though in truth, it might have been someone else in the hierarchy of the church.

> A certain Pope rose well before dawn, as was his custom, and said his morning prayers and read some scriptures. He then went to the kitchen and picked up a cup of coffee and his spiral-bound steno notepad. He took his coffee and notepad into the Papal Garden to enjoy the morning air. The birds sang, the air was cool as the sky brightened, and slowly the

sun's disk broke over the crest of the eastern mountains and ascended above the horizon. The Pope looked in wonder at this marvelous sight, then thought for a moment and wrote in his notebook, "solus in orientum ascendas." (The sun rises in the east). You must forgive my attempt at Latin.

At noontime, the Pope again went out into the garden with a sandwich in hand, and his spiral bound steno notepad under his arm. The sun's warmth enveloped him as he looked skyward, thought for a minute shaking off the sun's glare, and wrote in his notebook, "solus altissimus est." (The sun is at its highest).

The pattern was repeated in the evening with a cup of cappuccino, and his notebook under his arm. He looked this time to the west as the sun slowly settled below the western horizon. He was dazzled by the brilliant orange colors among the scattered clouds. He wrote in his book, "solus in occidentium descendas." (The sun is setting in the west). He thought for a few days about what he had observed. Then it struck him, "Eurekibus" he said, "the earth is at center of the universe." "The sun revolves about the earth, this shall be canon law."

While the story might not be actual fact, it portrays how the assumption of the earth being the center of the universe could very well have occurred. This mythical Pope made some observations and came to an erroneous conclusion, based on his view of the sun from a single point on earth.

Copernicus, and Galileo after him, looked at the heavens from a different perspective. They looked at the sun and the planets as if they were sitting in space observing what was going on. Based on their observations of planetary movements, and self-questioning of the alternatives, they concluded that in fact, the sun was at the center of the solar system and the earth revolved about the sun. Galileo made the mistake of publishing his findings and was declared a heretic for daring to contradict the church's official position on the matter. Galileo loved his church and was devoted to it. He never intended to stir up controversy, only to share what he had learned. His church felt that its pronouncements were infallible and unerring.

I told this next story to my fellow choir singers, and afterward said, "Now there is a test." I asked one alto, "How fast are you traveling right now?" She looked at me with wide eyes, as if I were crazy, and without pushing her further, since the question was rhetorical, I explained that in Colorado the approximate circumference of the earth is about 20,000 miles, give or take a thousand or two. I said, we make this trip in 24 hours as the earth rotates about its axis. Dividing the 20,000-mile trip by 24 hours, we find that all Coloradans are traveling at about 833 miles per hour.

From our chairs our perspective is that we are not moving at all. We protest the notion that we are traveling faster than the speed of sound. I explained that the reason you don't feel you are traveling that fast is that the chair you sit on is also going the same speed, as is the church you're in, as is the city and state you live in. You have zero speed relative to your surroundings, but not relative to the axis of the earth.

Another choir member raised his hands and said, "You have it all wrong." We revolve about the sun once every year, 8,760 hours. That trip is about 584 million miles. Simple arithmetic shows that we are traveling at an average speed of about 66,000 miles per hour.

A third choir member said, "wait you don't understand." We are traveling away from the source of the Big Bang at probably 10 percent of the speed of light. "That's about 18,000 miles per second.

You can see that, depending upon the perspective you take, you will get a different answer to the original question, "How fast are you traveling." Our mythical Pope assumed, based on his observations that the sun was revolving about the earth. He could not see that it was he who was traveling, not the sun, as the earth rotated about its axis.

When any church leader takes an attitude that he or she knows for sure what God is about and what is truth, dissent and danger follow. We all must be humble in the sight of God, because His knowledge and actions are unfathomable to us. We must take the time to look at any issue from more than one perspective; otherwise we may fall far wide of our mark. It is not wise to quote scripture (whether Bible, Koran, Book of Mormon or any similar source) as a blanket authoritative basis for our actions on earth. There may be more than one interpretation of the source material and the scriptural writer may have been expressing himself quite differently from that which we assume.

The church of the Middle Ages first took an attitude that it was the fount of all knowledge, and second, once it took a position, it was heretical to contradict it. This was a rigid dictate that has never quite died a respectable death.

Mankind has typically claimed a more important position for itself than it really should. In the Moses era the world was small. It went as far as Rome to the northwest and Egypt to the south. There was no North or South America, or North Pole or South Pole. Asia, if it were known, would have seemed to be a million miles away. The Middle East was it, that's where life was. The people that lived there were important. God was dealing with a very small number of people. Now we have six billion people on earth, but most of us see ourselves as part of a much smaller grouping. We may see ourselves as a unique part of a family, church, tribe, corporation, city, or a nation.

We should not expect ourselves to be the sole occupants of space. Carl Sagan, the late astronomer and author of the Cosmos Television series and book of the same name estimated that there could be as many planets in the Milky Way galaxy as stars. He estimated that there could have been, or will be, as many as one billion planets upon which a technical civilization arose, or will arise, at one time or another. Taking our experience on earth, that a technical civilization has existed only one millionth of the time the planet existed, he concluded that there may be as few as ten other intelligent civilizations existing today in our galaxy. However, multiply this by the estimated 100 billion galaxies that are believed to exist and one sees that the probability of other intelligent life existing is quite high.

Whether other forms of intelligent life look like us is a moot point. The point is that our God is probably the God of many more beings than the six billion on our planet. We cannot look upon ourselves as important in a numerical or tribal sense. Yet we are important to God. He knows us by name. We cannot fall to the ground without His knowledge. This should teach us a little humility, because we are such a very small part of his kingdom.

Tribalism

The Prophet Muhammad grew up in a tribal culture. His guardian uncle Abu Talib was an influential leader of the Banu Hashim clan within the Quarish tribe in Mecca. Tribes were close-knit groups of people in the first millennium that were fiercely self-protecting. Muhammad was a just and devout man, wishing to restore to Muslims the original monotheistic religion of Abraham and Moses. He was also a political and military leader who waged war against the Meccans and ultimately defeated them. He had those who had earlier mocked him for his religious beliefs, executed when they were captured. He referred to those who worshipped many gods as infidels and justified their deaths.

The Koran includes rules and laws for believing Muslims, much like the Torah included rules for the tribal Jewish peoples. The writings reflected, in part, the environment and culture of the day.

Today we interpret life based on the culture in which we live and work. In the corporate executive culture, those of importance look towards being awarded stock options or "retention bonuses" as a natural reward of business. These people surround themselves with persons of like mind, but do not see people in abject circumstances caused by the practices of their corporations. If we align ourselves only with our own tribe we will be imprisoned by a lack of perspective, and will not see the reality of life.

Many of us think of tribalism in the past, however it exists today. There are tribes in Afghanistan, Africa, Central and South America, but also in major cities around the world wearing gray business suits. These tribes consist of self-protecting men, primarily, who guard their self-interests very closely. They influence elected government officials by providing money to fund their campaigns. In return they expect treatment that will guard their opulent and extravagant life styles.

Religion must go beyond the bounds of tribalism to even contemplate the nature of the loving God. The Spirit is not captive to the tribe. Whether you think tribes disappeared long ago, the basic instincts of earlier tribes remain in our culture. Tribes are self-interest groups dedicated to the welfare of its members. Muhammad, when he dictated the Koran to someone who could write, was influenced to some extent by his sense of tribalism, because he lived within that culture. We too in America see spiritual values with tainted vision because we are members of tribes, be they work, political, or church-related.

Importance and Investiture

Many people and institutions of power think of themselves as being important. The Evil One offered Jesus a position of power, if He would but fall down and worship him. Jesus would have none of this. He did not want or need power, He had it, but used His position as a servant, not a king.

The Church of Constantine gradually thought of itself as important once it gained acceptance and power. With power ultimately came corruption. Once officially established as the state religion of the Roman Empire the church felt that its importance exceeded that of the state. It felt that it could appoint and crown kings, start inquisitions and religious wars, forgive sins, and burn heretics at the stake. The church built a hierarchy that was invested with power. Because the church felt that its Pope, and he alone, was the direct emissary of God, that position was invested with the highest power on earth.

The church of tomorrow cannot repeat these mistakes again. It must remain humble in the sight of God. Jesus taught that the first must be last. That is, those in power must be servants of all. This is the model for the important, that they must look at themselves as unimportant. Only God is important.

Power is no longer restricted to the church, but is foremost in politics and the corporate world. With power and investiture comes a distancing of the powerful from the powerless. A depersonalization process takes place. Power forms a barrier to reality and change, but it does not have to be so. Giving up one's invested power or position, is a sacrifice, but not of the magnitude of Jesus' sacrifice. One must change glasses to see the possibilities by using power for the common good, not the personal good. Jesus' message to me is that those in power must take the role of servants. I believe the New Testament is very clear on this. Society needs people to hold positions of power, but they must act for the common good.

The deep recession of 2008-09 caused the mass of American people to be incensed by the greed of the corporate elite to reward themselves with the bailout money supplied by the taxpayers. The corporate elite felt entitled to retention bonuses and expensive perks because they did not feel the least bit accountable for the collapse of the finance industry, nor did they feel accountable to the people who paid their salaries. They certainly did not feel accountable for the pain of those they made unemployed or homeless.

Tradition

The church of the fourth century based its canonical beliefs on antiquity, authenticity, universality, and accepted tradition. That is, it accepted scripture that was as close to Jesus, or to eyewitness followers of Jesus, as much as possible. The Bishops also went with the oldest writings that existed. Finally, they accepted the views and practices most universally accepted in the churches of that time.

Tradition can be comforting to people in society, particularly when it reinforces a positive value system. People don't like change for the most part, other than fashion designers or car designers who rely upon, and create change for the benefit of their industry. People in religion have never seemed to welcome change. How many times have we heard the phrase, "We've always done it this way before."

However, tradition can be a barrier to receiving and acknowledging new information, and understanding the metaphorical passages in the Scriptures as spiritual messages rather than categorical facts. Since we human beings dislike change, tradition can also be a barrier to re-looking at our various liturgies and our music to see what appropriate changes might be made to bring our worship into consistence with historical reality. We must decode the metaphors of the early church so that their messages are made clear for modern religious people.

The tradition that women are excluded from the Roman Catholic clergy and that male clergy must be celibate is a long-standing practice that must be challenged, because the basis for these positions is not realistic, practical, or based on sound biblical positions. The argument that church law does not permit changes to these traditions is a millstone around the neck of the church. The fact that the church "has always done it this way" does not make a practice valid, reasonable, or beneficial.

Luke emphasizes the importance of women in his gospel and their prominence as being supportive of Jesus' ministry every bit as much as the twelve. Tradition unfortunately will be the big barrier to change.

The Failure to Say I'm Wrong

In society, it is crucial that people be willing to say, "I was wrong, or we were wrong." To say, "I was wrong" is to admit that life is more important than me. There is nothing wrong about admitting a mistake. Americans respond positively to admissions of mistakes, but may generalize a single failure to admit a mistake to include everything a person of power says as false. Americans have gone through two presidential terms where the administration failed to admit they were wrong. They held to incorrect positions and lied to the people. The populace is not dumb it will ultimately find truth.

Certainty

Most of us like to feel certain of our positions and viewpoints. We don't like to say we were wrong. The Bible is something we can ascribe certainty to. We can say that it was certainly dictated by God to the people of the day. Therefore, if God has dictated the Bible, it must be factually true. From this platform it is easy to memorize sections of it that we can later recite as factual truths.

Spiritual giants tend to say "I don't know much for sure except my sense of the presence of God in my life." God made mankind in His own image, but man has also formed an image of God, and worships that image. We have similarly put God in a box to fit our world, made him a male to fit our patriarchal mentality, and put Him in a timescale to fit our calendar. This helps us have some degree of certainty about our position in the universe. Our God, however, is a mystery. He gives evidence of His existence and of His marvelous works. He is unknowable and way beyond our ability to understand Him. He has shown us through the Hubble telescope the incredible universe He is creating before our very eyes.

As I write this paragraph I am listening to Bach's B Minor Mass. What an incredible piece of music and expression of God's great majesty. What a tremendous gift of composition did God bestow on this German musician. We have only to look around us to see what God has done. Nonetheless, we must discard the certainty of our positions to the faith and trust we must take in His positions. Paul made it clear that our trust in God will save us, not our certainty in our own positions.

The People Cage

There are many other cage-like constraints that add to people's myopia. Education, or lack thereof, environment, limited parenting are some others. I've discussed a few, but surely these constraints are real, just like the wires that confine a bird in its cage. Just as the bird can see beyond the wires that constrain it, so we also must see beyond our constraints and those forces that may tend to distort truth. If society is to be free, it must guard truth at all costs. Similarly, people must look past the barriers of time, language, culture, tribalism, tradition, and investiture to see truth. We must always gain perspective by seeing issues from more than one vantage point. We, as laypeople, must demand truth and put on new glasses that will give us the far-sightedness to see the world as it really is.

CHAPTER 2

GRASPING THE WIND

God is like the wind. The wind cannot be seen,
but we can see the effects of it.

My Greatest lesson

I learned what I believe was my greatest lesson in the eighth grade. I saw a picture of the ladder of generality in my English book. Specifics and details were placed on the bottom rung while principles and generalities were placed on the top rung. I've carried that image all my life and it has helped me keep clear in my mind to separate the big picture from the microscopic view. As an engineer, I've always thrived on solving problems. I've observed in life that people seem to try to solve problems at the detail end of the ladder, when they should be first looking at the top end, and then working themselves into details after grasping the larger picture.

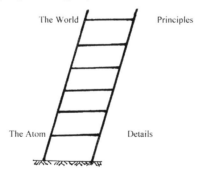

The Ladder of Generality
Figure 2.1

What tends to separate us in religion is details. These are unimportant in contrast with the principles that God would have us understand. There would be far fewer denominations and sects if we could come closer to agreeing on principles. As you read this book, I would ask you always to stay focused on the big picture. This, perhaps, is especially true in religion.

How the Ancients Experienced God

There is a vast difference in what the ancients knew and what we know today. We have information available at a keystroke. The ancients learned either by experience or folklore. Those of us who have lived in the 20th and 21st centuries have been taught that if something is real one should be able to see, touch, and feel it. As we know, this isn't quite true. Physicists cannot see or touch an atom, or a quark, or a meson. They can however, see evidence of their existence by the trails they leave when atoms collide. Reality then, is neither proved nor disproved by our ability to see anything in three dimensions. So it is with God. The Spirit is not seen, but it leaves evidence of its being.

The ancient Hebrews had a concept of a three-tiered universe. The heavens, and stars were above the clouds in what was referred to as the "firmament." The sun and moon passed through six windows each in the east and west sides of the firmament. Rain came through other windows in the firmament. The gods lived above the firmament. At the ground level, which floated on water, were humans, plants, and animals. Below this were the fiery furnaces of hell.

The ancient pagans made representations of the gods with stone so that they could see and touch them, and therefore bring reality to them. Monotheists and pagans alike expected that God or the gods dwelt in the Heavens and were unseen and unknowable. They had to have believed that the deities were responsible for fertility and good harvests and victories in war. They obviously felt that the gods were looking upon them and rewarding or punishing them according to their behavior. They offered sacrifices in order to influence the gods to provide them the things they needed.

One of my favorite Bible stories is the contest between Elijah and the prophets of Baal on Mt. Carmel as told in 1 Kings 18:20-ff. The prophets had prepared their sacrifice and were yelling toward the heavens to have their god send down fire to burn the sacrifice. This went on for a number of hours without success so Elijah mocked them by suggesting they yell louder because their god might be hunting, on a journey, or perhaps asleep. This story, to me, was a great example of satire. It illustrates the mentality of early pagans.

The story writer went on to describe how God not only sent fire to devour Elijah's offering, but the fire also devoured the water that had been poured around the altar and the very stones from which the altar was built. The end of the story describes that the followers of Elijah killed every last one of the Baalites. Mendelssohn captured this story in his famous oratorio, *Elijah.*

The story is very dramatic and expresses a very wide divergence of outcomes of the worship of Baal and of God. The point being made was that idolatry leads only to death, whereas the worship of God leads to overwhelming abundance. If the story is taken literally, one might believe that God is bloodthirsty and vengeful. To me, the story is about a comparison of outcomes between an idolater and a faithful worshipper of God. The story is not about vengeance, but about the abundance that God provides to those who trust Him.

People of all cultures believed that the one or more gods they worshipped had miraculously created the earth and heavens. Each culture had its own creation story. Each seemed to have a sense of sacrifice to please their god(s). I suspect they all looked to the heavens when offering prayers that they hoped the gods would hear.

What has come to us from the earliest religions were these concepts:
1. God was "up there" (in the heavens)
2. God was our creator
3. We were dependent on God for everything
4. God could be influenced by our sacrifices
5. God could hear our prayers
6. Gods have a gender; primarily male, but some were female

We've cast away the concepts of polytheistic worship that the pagans had. Monotheism has won and is universally accepted today. What people fail to see today, however, are the unseen idols that they worship; power, wealth, fame, and beauty come to mind.

The Judeo-Christian religion carried most of these six concepts into the beginnings of the Christian faith. The fact that churches today have spires or towers that reach upward gives credence to the concept that God is "up there." Sadly, this architectural concept points in the wrong direction. To me, God should be thought of as "in here," not "out there." We see God in people, and in what they do and who they are. Perhaps a sphere or a circle is a better symbol than a spire.

Symbolism

We accept God as the creator of the universe and the provider of all things that we need. Let us look at some of the concepts that have come to us from very early religion.

I looked at a Baltimore Catechism published by the Roman Catholic Church many years ago, and in it I saw a picture of a child walking toward a church and at the back door there was a ladder reaching into the clouds. The symbolism was clear in that the child reaches heaven through the church. Unfortunately, I also saw it as a symbol that God wasn't in the church, but somewhere else. This symbol also gave the church a focus of importance and power, which I believe it carries today. The symbol may have given a clear picture to a child, but I think the church could have designed a better image, perhaps of joining a circle of people within the church.

Sacrifice

The Jews sacrificed animals; the Mayans sacrificed people. The Mayans would sacrifice captives from other tribes or young females from among their own. So that God would be pleased, the purest of sacrifices had to be made. That meant unmarried virgins were selected rather than older adults. The high priests obviously were attracted to the young virgins, so they assumed that their God would also, and therefore, would be pleased. Here, the priests ascribed to God the value system they held as their own. Does this make sense? Is God's perspective the same as mankind's? I don't think so. We should not be trapped into assuming that. When I think of God's pronouncement to do justice and love mercy, I feel that the Mayan religion flunked on both counts with its concept of sacrifice.

I don't know what other cultures did in other parts of the world, but it is clear that sacrifice grew up independently around the world and was a means of influencing the gods. Sacrifice grew as a means to influence a bountiful harvest, or assure fertility, or protection from enemies.

In our cultures today, sacrifice is essentially practiced as a fasting. Some cultures still sacrifice animals. While I was a working engineer, a colleague showed me a video of construction workers in Africa killing a lamb and spreading its blood upon the ground where foundations for a gold mine were to be constructed. Most of us would treat this ritual as superstition rather than a proper rite.

To me the concept of Jesus as a sacrificial lamb is a carry-over from Jewish tradition and a further carry-over from pagan practices. I doubt that God demanded atonement in the form of blood from Jesus or any other individual in exchange for the forgiveness of sins. I believe this demeans God's willingness to forgive in response to repentance. I can see how the concept of sacrifice crept into the Christian religion, since it was such a part of Jewish practice.

The symbology of sacrifice is that giving begets receiving. When giving back to God, one does not give miserly. What is the greatest gift one can give, one's life, of course? What comes back to mankind? New life through the resurrection. I believe the message we should receive from Jesus' death was the utter extent He was willing to go to sacrifice himself for His people. God is not bloodthirsty, and there is no payment that would satisfy His desire to have a loving relationship with those who choose to love Him. Jesus' death was a choice He, himself made in order to show His people, He loved them, and the extent to which they must be willing to give of themselves to show God's love for mankind. The sacrifice should never be perceived as a "payment" in my mind. The sacrifice as such, was to give mankind new life.

Jesus spoke of the wealthy contributing to the temple tax out of their abundance, but the widow who gave two coins of minimal value, gave more than the wealthy, because she gave all that she had. She sacrificed, the others didn't.

In a different vein, consider that for there to be a resurrection, Jesus had to die. Not only did Jesus die, but also subsequently he walked among his disciples and ate with them. The emphasis for me is that Jesus' death pointed to new life, not to a payment for sin.

The Israelites carried on the practice of sacrifice into the Christian era, but changed its meaning from that understood by pagans. The Israelites understood that they had a special covenant relationship with God. As such, they felt they had to be ritually clean and set apart from the cultures of the day. They understood sacrifice to have two parts; one was for atonement of sins and praise to God, the other was to provide sustenance for the Levite priests. Sacrifice was no longer meant to influence the gods, but to acknowledge wrongdoing and to appear pure before their Maker. Their sins, therefore, were ceremonially put upon the animals they sacrificed, and the death of the animal washed away their sin. Unlike the Mayans, who may have sacrificed people they had captured, the Israelites sacrificed from the abundance that God had provided them. They acknowledged that they had come from God and belonged to Him.

The Book of Leviticus sets out the five types of offerings (sacrifices) that were recognized under the Laws of Moses. These were:

Burnt Offerings   - an act of praise and adoration to God
Cereal Offerings   - a sacrifice of atonement and praise
Peace Offering   - a covenant meal shared by the people and a priest where the worshipper was sacramentally related to God.
Sin Offering   - an offering that was made when the worshipper had inadvertently broken one of God's laws.
Guilt Offering   - an act that included restitution to the victim plus a twenty percent increase paid to the temple.

Each of these offerings required the sacrifice of an animal, bird, or grain product, part of which was consumed by fire and part of which was to be consumed by the priests. In all cases, the priest sprinkled the blood of the animal on the sides of the altar. Blood was considered the essence of life, and therefore was holy.

The odors from the fire were intended to be pleasing to God. Grain offerings were sprinkled with frankincense to enhance the aroma of the burning offering. It had to have been in the mind of the priests that God could literally smell the odors emanating from the burning sacrifices.

When a sin was committed intentionally, there was no offering that could atone for the act under Jewish law. According to priestly tradition, such as person was to be cut off from the people. An example of such a case is found in Numbers 15:30 wherein a man was caught gathering wood on the Sabbath during the exodus in the wilderness. The priests arrested the man and brought him to Moses and Aaron asking what they should do. The Biblical writer wrote that God said he should be stoned to death. A few verses later, Moses was commanded by God to have the people make tassels of blue and append them to their clothes to remind them to obey God's commandments and to be holy.

Stoning, which was the means of execution by the Hebrew community, was intended to keep evil from infecting the people. Execution was a corporate act of banishing evil, not an act of individual revenge.

The justice system of the day seemed to be black and white. There was no jail time, nor free lunches while in prison. People were permanently excommunicated from society for mocking God and sinning in defiance of God. It seems that punishment for sinning on the Sabbath, which was to be holy, exceeded willful sinning at other times. On other days, sin was judged on the principle of "an eye for an eye, a tooth for a tooth." The principle here was not literal in a sense, but that the limits of punishment should not exceed the seriousness of the crime.

It is perhaps little wonder that the tradition of severe punishment followed from the Israelites to other parts of the world. Brutal punishments were a way of keeping the people in line and purging what might have been considered evil elements out of society.

My reading of the Hebrew Bible is that the people experienced God through their leaders; Moses, Abraham, and the prophets. God was expressed as being merciful to the Hebrew people, bailing them out of trouble time and again. They also saw God as being intolerant of sin and being unmerciful to the heathen. This theme carries into the Koran.

The writers of the Hebrew Bible painted a picture of a God who was intent on having a holy people to worship Him. He was intolerant of sin and backsliding, and punished Israel for its sins. When God deemed it necessary, He gave power to the enemies of the Israelites to conquer them in war. He also gave the Israelites power over others as they were led to the Promised Land. The mighty and powerful right hand of God was surely portrayed in the Hebrew Scriptures.

I see that the ancients experienced God through historical events that impacted them as a people and amazed them. Since most people were illiterate, they relied on the priesthood and prophets to interpret God's acts, and the laws and commandments handed down to them. This tradition follows to the current era although now, the people are literate.

The Presence of God

If the Mayans and the pagans perceived as God dwelling "up there," then the Hebrews thought of Him as closer, actually visiting them. Obviously, the writer of the creation story conceived of God as walking with Adam and Eve in the Garden. He was present with mankind. Later, we read that God was present on Mount Sinai in the burning bush when he appeared to Moses. He reached out to mankind and gave them the Ten Commandments as a way to stabilize their civilization.

In Genesis Chapter 15 the Biblical writer writes about God appearing to Abraham and establishing a covenant with him that he would be the father of many nations. That covenant was to be sealed by the rite of male circumcision. All through the Torah we read of God's presence among the Israelite leaders, Jacob, Joseph, Moses and others. God spoke to this one and to that one. When Joseph was sold by his brothers to be a slave in Egypt, God was shown to have made good come out of an evil act. God had saved a remnant of the Hebrew nation in Egypt during the seven years of famine in Judea so that their covenant relationship could be maintained.

God's angel spoke to Moses throughout his life and gave him the power to lead the Israelite people out of Egypt through the Sea of Reeds into the Promised Land. God continued His relationship with the Israelites through the prophets and leaders of the period of the kings. This is the substance of the Hebrew Bible that God was actively involved with His people.

How Modern Man Experiences God

When we read the Hebrew Bible we see the saving acts of God that took place over a thousand years compressed into 39 canonical books comprising about 1,100 pages. In that context, God would have appeared to be active on every page with few exceptions. Today, we live in real time and we become quite unaware of God's continuing saving acts. We see evil and suffering in our world and wonder if God is alive. What we experience today is no different from that which the Israelites experienced. Their timescale was our timescale. Their perspective was as restricted as ours.

God is very much alive and active in our world. He brings about change on His timescale, not ours. He continues to take the works of the Evil One and transforms them into ultimate good. We see this only in hindsight.

How then can we see the works of God? I see this in four ways:
- Through nature
- Through the works of other people
- Through our personal experiences with Him
- Through the works of society

God as Experienced in Nature

We do not see the wind, but we feel its pressure and see the clouds that are carried by it. We know it exists, even though, by itself, it is not visible. Our first evidence of God's presence is in the sky. We see the universe, or at least that part that is visible to us. With the help of the Hubble telescope we can look far out into space, and far back into time. We see incredible views, breathtaking in magnitude and glory. What we can see is indescribable. The Biblical writers never saw these images, nor could they have comprehended them, yet they experienced God in their own way.

One summer night in 1953, I laid on the deck of a troop ship headed for Korea while in the middle of the Pacific Ocean and seeing a million or more stars in the night sky. What indescribable beauty and majesty. I was probably looking out at a distance of many light-years, and also looking back in time many hundreds of thousands of years. These views are not the product of an accident of science, but of the mere thought and act of an unknowable God. That was a small view of God's works, something few of us see. What we see with the naked eye is only an infinitesimal fraction of the Milky Way galaxy to which we belong. This galaxy is only one of 100 billion other galaxies flying off into space. Our universe is incomprehensible, yet it is in the beginning phase of creation.

Scientists talk of the Big Bang event, when all of the matter of the universe was tightly compressed into a single small sphere such that even atoms could not move nor light escape. Then it exploded, and as it did, the laws of physics were born and the universe we see was being created. I have long asked myself, "Was this tiny ball stable?" If stable, what caused it to become unstable and so explode and expand? What preceded this event? Science doesn't have an answer for this question, but there had to have been a "before." Logically it could have been a "Big Crunch," where an earlier universe had collapsed upon itself as in a massive black hole in which gravity is so strong that not even light particles escape from its pull. Philosophically, we find it difficult to imagine a universe governed by a timeless and all-powerful God.

Look at grass or perennial flowers. They bloom brightly in the warm summer and are nourished by the rains. In the winter the grass and the flowers are dormant, sleeping as it were, and waiting for the spring rains before they arise to new life. Jesus said, "Consider the lilies of the field. Is there anything so beautiful, yet they neither toil nor spin?" The caterpillar creeps along and then one day it becomes a beautiful butterfly. Young saplings grow to become mature trees spreading their branches to provide shade for life below. Over time the tree ages and weakens, disease takes its toll, and the tree dies, making room for more new young saplings to take its place. Nature provides us innumerable examples of youth, maturity, decay and death in the plant world, but life always returns. God shows us these cycles that are models for the human life cycle.

In the animal world we see mothers who bear young, feed and protect them and as they mature, then teach them the means of survival. We as humans, for the most part, follow these models when rearing our own young. Ultimately, they replace us.

God as Experienced through Others

I'm a music lover, particularly of baroque and sacred music. I enjoy the music of Bach, Handel, Vivaldi, Gabrielli, and others. I am particularly moved when I listen to Bach's B Minor Mass, or his St. Matthew Passion. The Air for the G String and his piece "Come, Sweet Death" are to me awesome compositions. The Requiems of Brahms, Faure, and Mozart are similarly very moving. I see God's hand in the creation of all these pieces and many more by other composers. God did not dictate the pieces note by note, but certainly these composers were inspired by God and given the gifts to create this heavenly music.

I see beauty and the Hand of God in the art of DaVinci and Michelangelo among others. How beautiful was the portrayal in the Sistine Chapel of God's hand reaching out to touch Adam? As God had inspired scriptural writers, so also has He inspires composers, artists, sculptors, scientists, and others to create masterpieces.

God is present in the positions that many people took against slavery and other injustices to our fellow men. Abraham Lincoln, of course, gets the majority of credit for his stand for the abolition of slavery. Many before him, however, also took that stand.

Rosa Parks and Martin Luther King Jr. stood up against the injustices toward African American blacks. Others stood with them against prejudice and segregation and the attitudes that some whites took that they were 'superior" to their black brothers. If we all look back a few million years, we were all descended from black Africans who lived in caves or in trees. Our blackness was merely nature's way of protecting us from the sun's ultraviolet rays. Blackness had nothing to do with superiority or inferiority. When the human race moved into the Temperate Zone climate, blackness no longer was necessary and the people ultimately, over millennia, lost their blackness and became white.

Jesus obviously brought a new worldview to the first century Jews and their gentile neighbors. He raised the bar of human behavior and brought with Him the means by which the kingdom of Heaven could be experienced on earth.

If we look closely at the people around us we can see God at work through them. They may be average men and women, but when you see their acts of goodness and sacrifice, you know God is not far away. Consider the works of Mother Teresa, for one, or David Livingston for another. How many servicemen gave their lives in past wars to save the lives of their comrades? These men and women gave the ultimate sacrifice not in payment for anything, but as a gracious gift. God's spirit does live within others and us, and we see the evidence of that presence in the acts of others. The symbolism of church spires pointing to the sky is comically wrong. God lives within us, if we are open to His presence. God is not out where the spires point, but within us. We can know this if we but listen to His still small voice that resides in our minds.

God as Experienced in Our Own Lives

How do we experience God in direct communication with us? When I shave and look in the mirror, I've never seen a shining halo surrounding my head. God is not giving me dictation as I put these thoughts to paper. My experience with God is with a "still small voice" speaking to me in my own voice. Positive thoughts come to me and I recognize the thoughts as good. I contrast these with selfish thoughts that also come to me. These are the suggestions from the Evil One. Whether I am fed suggestions from an angel, the Holy Spirit, or God Himself, I am satisfied they come from God. In all circumstances, I never hear orders or commands, but only ideas.

Whether it was the Angel Gabriel that spoke to Muhammad giving him instruction to write the Koran, I don't know. I am convinced that God did give Muhammad the substance of the Koran, whether by dictation or by other means does not matter to me. I believe that the Biblical scriptures were similarly provided, not by dictation, but by the still small voice of inspiration and the manner by which people experienced God's presence and actions.

This was the way Jesus came to Israel, not as a powerful military commander with a thunderous voice, but as a helpless infant. As a teacher, he spoke with loving compassion to His children in a calm, quiet voice. He reached out to the marginalized and gave them hope and encouragement. He had an impact on those who came into His presence and amazed people who really listened to Him.

So it is with God. He comes to us with a quiet, still voice. He does not give orders. He does not give dictation. He gives ideas and advice. It is for the listener to choose to follow or reject that advice.

God as Experienced in The Works of Society

I believe God does act in society, but I have a hard time recognizing how and when it happens. We can assume that God is present in natural disasters, but I have a hard time believing that He causes them. He certainly is present when people mobilize and reach out to the victims of such tragedies as hurricanes, earthquakes, and similar disasters. When plagues and disease ravage large populations, I don't believe God is the cause, but I believe that He is present in the nurturing and healing given by others. God does not start wars in my opinion, but He must be present with the winner, for His own reasons.

Does He cause economic injustice? Hardly, the Evil One is behind that. God reaches out to individuals to point out the injustices so that others might be spurred to correct them. The current economic downturn of 2008-10 is an example. The downturn was a result of greed, competition, and self-serving individuals and corporations. God, however, can make that event an opportunity for change and economic justice.

So, I do see that God acts in society, but not necessarily every single act of nature that may result in death or homelessness. The path of the Israelite nation was torturous. The Israelites suffered hardship. They were made captive. Their goods were stripped from them by their conquerors. Even with this hardship, a remnant always remained faithful and God stood by them shaping their society to make it better.

In our society today we see examples of good. We have a medical institution that has dedicated itself to making life better and longer for many people. It cares about the sick and offers healing to both those who can afford it and to those that cannot.

Society has created an educational system wherein our young are taught to think and to expand their knowledge and capabilities. We have an agricultural industry that feeds the world. We have industries that have developed vehicular travel and air travel so that we might see the world or more easily connect with loved ones separated by distance. We have a communications industry that allows us to share thoughts and ideas beyond our small neighborhoods. All these things and more have ultimately been gifts of God made through the workings of his creatures.

The development of laws and a judicial system has brought order out of chaos in society over the years. Through laws we can legislate a system of behavior that brings some sense of justice and fairness in our culture. When laws are applied to all people uniformly and without prejudice, then we have social justice.

The Questions I ask myself about God

Why is God Not Visible?

I've sat through many sermons that I never heard. Rather, I would drift into thought about God. I would pose questions to myself and then try to find answers. One of these questions was, why God is not seen? He created life, the planets and the universe, I reasoned, then why did He choose not to reveal Himself? Is it because we are sinful and He is perfect, and therefore cannot be in the presence of sin? No, I concluded, He is well aware of sin and of the terrible deeds that people commit. Is it strictly because He is a spirit and we are physical beings living in a different dimension? This is plausible, but God could have chosen otherwise. God is love, I thought. What is it about love that would cause Him to secrete Himself from us? I searched for that quality of love that most nearly defines it.

Cold defines hot, I thought, short defines long, but what defines a quality such as love or hatred? God, I thought, would be so beautiful to us that we would be unalterably drawn to Him. What's wrong with that, I thought? I said, it takes away one of the main qualities that define love, that is *choice*. What can define love is the free choice of two people to commit themselves, one for the other. So it should be with God. He loves us, but He gives us the *choice* to love Him or reject Him. Choice, to me is one of the basic qualities that define love.

Trust is a similar quality that is necessary for a marriage to succeed and society to function. So also in a personal relationship, trust is also a defining quality. By not seeing God, we must put trust to work to cement the relation. By selecting *choice* and *trust* as basic qualities of love, I do not mean to exclude other qualities of caring, fidelity, giving, sharing, communicating, and when necessary, sacrificing.

We are not puppets on a set of strings. He could govern us that way, but that would not be love, it would be manipulation. That would give God no satisfaction. He is Love. He makes Himself vulnerable to our rejection. If we accept Him sight unseen, He will be pleased because we trusted Him.

It takes us a while to get to know God, but at some point He wants a commitment from us. This is not a mechanical "I do" in church, but a commitment of the heart. What gifts do we give to God? The gifts He treasures are not pious acts or sacrifices of animals, but acts of good will to others. As Jesus said, "feed the hungry, care for the widow, reach out to the marginalized and love your neighbor as yourself." If we choose to love God, we will do His works and will be obedient to what He whispers in our ear. We love God whom we do not see, by loving and caring for those whom we do see.

If you can buy this viewpoint, then membership in a particular religion is of no account. A mechanical commitment is not a main concern. It must be an individual commitment of the heart, that perhaps is made silently, but is sealed with a promise to listen for, and hear God, and to do His will.

Is God Exclusive?

I cannot believe so. God is neither Christian, nor Jew, Muslim, Buddhist, nor member of any other sect. These are man-made divisions of understanding and worshipping God. None of them are the unique doorway to a relationship or future life with God.

Jesus could have been born into a Mayan culture, or into a Chinese culture or within an African tribe. He wasn't. That fact does not exclude Mayans, Eskimos, and African tribal people from the love of God. They also are His children, and as such, are entitled to be part of the Kingdom of Heaven, if they choose to hear and be obedient to their Maker.

When we point to the Bible as a basis for exclusive membership in the Kingdom of Heaven, we do so selfishly and erroneously, not understanding the magnitude of our dimensionless God. It is unfortunate that some religious groups feel they are an exclusive group having the sole keys to the Kingdom. By having this mentality, people exalt themselves to positions of importance that is not justified. While we have a choice to have a relationship with God, He also chooses whom He will save and whom he will not save. As Luther and Calvin taught, we are saved by God's grace and free choice, not by our works or sense of self-importance. I suspect that many who feel that they are part of an exclusive group to be in the Kingdom will end up saying, "Lord, Why have you forsaken me?" Be humble in the sight of God.

What Do We Understand About God?

Is He the same today as yesterday? This is the first question I dealt with in my youth. Is God different today than He was 2,000 – 3,000 years ago? That is to say, did God do magic in biblical days, and then stop doing this kind of thing after Jesus died?

Some Christian scholars in the 1950s and 60s posed the thought that God had died, figuratively speaking. My conclusion is that God is the same today as He was forever in the past. He created the laws of nature, and He has not, nor will not, abrogate those laws. We need this assurance. God has made Himself predictable to us this way. He does not abruptly shut off gravity otherwise we would all fly off into space. Did people live to be 900 years old way back when? No, they probably had a life span somewhat shorter than ours. Is the book of Genesis wrong and is God a liar? God is not a liar. The writer of Genesis expressed himself or herself in the concepts of that day.

Does God Perform Magic?

No, God does not perform magic. Did Jesus really perform miracles? No, I don't believe that Jesus performed miracles in the literal sense that we understand today. Jesus performed things that were of a miraculous quality to those who wrote about Him. He did not change water into fine wine. These are metaphors for the miraculous changes He made in the hearts and lives of people. The changes He brought were inexplicable to people of the day. They were miraculous in quality, but not scientifically. Does this make the Bible invalid, of course not? It is we who are myopic and shortsighted so as not to grasp the metaphorical meaning of these writings. The message of the Bible is as valid today as it was then, and just as important.

Jesus was fully human. He was bound by the same limitations that we have. He did not go through life crossing and uncrossing His fingers as he switched from being human to being God. He was sinless as a human being. For Jesus to conquer sin as God, and not a human, would in a sense be cheating. Jesus did not cheat. He did not do magic in the scientific sense. He made an unmistakable impact on people because He delivered a message that was totally foreign to the people of the day. He convinced people that God had a better way for them that could lead them to a kingdom of Heaven on earth. This was not a kingdom of military might and rule by power, but rather of love, kindness, and active reaching out to others.

Does God Interfere in Life?

Does God figuratively stand around with His hands in his pockets, while watching the world struggle and suffer? Smarter people than I have dealt with this question, and many books have been written on why God allows suffering. I believe that God wants the peoples of the world to be happy and to love and help one another. I believe He wants a just and fair society. I believe He does not want His people to suffer. I do not believe that God punishes people for their sins, but rather that suffering is the natural consequence of mankind choosing to listen and obey the Evil One in preference to God. It is the Evil One who brings suffering into the world, not God.

Suffering also comes as a result of the forces of nature. Tsunamis and hurricanes come and people are drowned. Earthquakes occur and people are crushed. Are these the acts of God? Again, I have to say no. God is not busy in Heaven pushing buttons manipulating our lives. Tectonic plates are still moving, ice ages have come and gone, and will come again. Rains fall and floods come. Lightning strikes and forest fires rage and people lose their homes. This is the world in which we live. Solving problems and overcoming difficulties are what makes mankind stronger and wiser. In that sense God shapes mankind and helps it survive with the forces of nature and of evil. God never takes away from man the choices or responsibilities that must be faced living on this planet.

Let me share a segment of my life where I felt God was involved, but did not manipulate. My first wife and I married while we were both in the service during the Korean War. We raised eight children while I put myself through college and started a career. She had been abandoned by her alcoholic parents and placed in a foster home by her grandfather. She believed her father had sexually abused her, and possibly he had. She had deeply repressed those memories. Her father died from his alcoholism before he was forty so he could never be confronted with that question.

She showed signs of schizophrenia early in the marriage and she alone, and we together, began therapy. Meanwhile, our children got into alcohol and became increasingly dysfunctional. This caused added stress to my wife and me.

When we moved from Massachusetts to Denver, she immediately felt she had lost her support system and started a series of eight nervous breakdowns over eight years requiring extensive in-patient hospitalization. She had undergone psychiatric counseling for 21 years by herself, and we together had seen at least two marriage counselors over 17 years. We also engaged the children in family counseling with us to try to recover some order and function within the family. Five of the children had become alcoholic and at least two got into marijuana. In spite of this, there was considerable love in the family and a sense of wanting to make things right.

After thirty-five years of marriage and the children starting to leave the nest, our counselor said to me, "You know Norm, some people choose to be sick." That rung a bell with me, and it wasn't too long before I dealt with a decision to stay or leave the marriage. This was precipitated when I first considered driving my car into a bridge abutment at sixty mph. As soon as I realized what I was thinking, I said that was not an answer. I then considered leaving the marriage, but faced the following alternatives:

1. My wife would commit suicide if I left (she had made one attempt previously).
2. She would get better
3. She would stay the same.

Could I live with all of the three alternatives? When I was comfortable that I could live with any of the three outcomes without guilt, I did leave the marriage. I left as a friend to my wife, and properly shared our joint assets so she would not suffer financially. My wife did not commit suicide, but did spend one solid year in the hospital under psychiatric care.

I became invested in another woman whom I had known and sung with for 10 years. We became engaged, but as we were discussing marriage plans, she was diagnosed with liver cancer. She survived six months, but during that time I was able to live with her and care for her. We had developed a deep love and affection in a fairly short time. I prayed to God that He would spare her, but He didn't. The night before she died, I finally asked God to take her and spare her any further suffering. Five hours later He did.

How did I look upon that whole adventure? I saw the Hand of God in it, but only in retrospect. I entered into a very unlikely divorce. I had vowed that I would never divorce, and would sacrifice to make the marriage last. I saw however that staying in an unhappy marriage was neither doing the family nor me any good. I did not get to marry my fiancée, but I was able to give her the love and care she so desperately wanted from her first marriage.

The children all overcame alcohol and made successes of themselves. They are all happy, functional, and contributors to society. My first wife died some fourteen years after the divorce, and she developed a support system, but never gave up her victim mentality. I married a widow about sixteen months after I lost my fiancée, and we have had a healthy and happy eighteen years together.

Did God cause my divorce? No, that was my choice. God may have whispered in my ear that I should consider it. If so, He did not disclose the ultimate consequences. I felt, however, that God used that event to draw me to a woman friend that would desperately need my love and care. For that, I am eternally grateful, as were my deceased fiancée and her children.

I could have considered that my fiancée's death was a punishment brought on me by God for my divorce. I don't. I don't see and worship a punitive God, I worship a loving and caring God who uses people (like me) to reach out to others whom He knows will need help and love.

Does God Answer Prayer?

Most of us are used to prayer to God with a series of requests. Please God, would you do this or that? He did not answer my prayer to spare my fiancée's life, but He did, to take it. We need to learn something from Jesus, who prayed, " not My will be done, but yours."

In prayer we give thanks and open our minds to His communication. I am sure He appreciates respect and gratitude for what He may do, unseen by us. Through others, He has given us food, clothing, housing, medicine, aviation, education, music and art, and all those tangible things that make our lives comfortable. He has given us partners, children and loved ones that delight us. He has given us churches: Monks and Ministers, Priests and Nuns, Rabbis and

Cantors, organists, scholars, teachers, and friends who provide for our spiritual nourishment and inspiration. He has given us love, wisdom, and freedom of choice. With all of this, He has given us the responsibility to manage all these gifts. These are the things we give thanks for.

Does God answer prayer? Yes, but too often we just don't understand how that answer comes. He knows our needs before we ask to have them fulfilled. He is way ahead of us. His actions are beyond our comprehension.

CHAPTER 3

THE EVIL ONE

If you have an enemy,
it is wise that you know him,
lest you become his victim.

I use the term "Evil One" for a reason. I came across a story about Josiah Plaistow from early colonial days in Boston when I was researching *The Whitcomb Family History,* a book I previously wrote. Josiah and his servants were caught stealing two bushels of corn from the local Indians. He was found guilty by the colonial government and for punishment, he was ordered to pay back the Indians double what he took from them. In addition, his servants were flogged for their part, and Mr. Plaistow was not to be referred to by his last name by anyone. He was to be called only "Josiah." That had to be a significant punishment in those days, to lose your name, so to speak. Consequently, I feel I do not wish to honor the Evil One by giving him a name.

How the Ancients Experienced Evil

There are probably are as many people in the world who believe in the Evil One as believe in God. The ancients certainly did. Satan, in the form of a serpent was part of the creation story, so treachery and evil were conceived to exist from the beginning. In the Garden of Eden Satan creates doubt in the mind of Eve concerning God's motive to forbid eating the fruit of the tree of good and evil. He then paints the picture of how good it would be if she did eat because she and Adam would become wise just like God. She became convinced and ultimately ate and had Adam eat the fruit also.

The creation myth indicates that the serpent was one of the many creatures made by God, but that he was quite sly and subtle. He could appear as an angel of light. His key characteristic was deception. God never gave him the power to force people to do evil, but only to suggest in deceptive ways that clouded reality in the minds of his victims. The writer of the Genesis story also pointed out that man's reaction to guilt is to blame someone else. Adam blamed

Eve, and Eve blamed the serpent. They both hid from God when they became aware of their nakedness. While the story portrayed physical nakedness, I suspect the writer was talking about man's spiritual transparency before God. God sees through us.

In the book of Job, God is described as saying to Satan what a good man Job was and how pleased He was with him. Satan then tested God by suggesting that Job was good only because he had prosperity. As we read the story, Job had ten children and thousands of animals and many servants. He was reported to be the wealthiest man in the east. He was also very devout in his worship and adoration of God. Satan essentially made a bet with God, that if God took away everything Job had, he would curse God. God allowed Satan to test Job on the condition that he could not harm him otherwise. Satan took everything that Job had away from him including his children, his animals, and his servants. He was left with nothing.

Job did not curse God, but stayed faithful to his Lord. Satan then upped the ante by asking permission to inflict Job with painful sores, head to toe. Still Job would not turn away from God. The story goes on to describe the discourses Job had with three friends who came to console him in his pain. They each suggested that surely Job should realize that God was punishing him in some way for offenses he may have unknowingly committed, or perhaps for his children's sins. Another suggested that Job was being punished for being self-righteous. Job argued with all his friends that he was innocent and blameless; nevertheless, he would accept God's actions for whatever reason God had.

After all the arguments had been laid out and Job had remained faithful to God, he was restored to health and given double the prosperity he once enjoyed. He again raised ten new children.

In this story Satan is portrayed as one of God's sons, a courtier in the heavenly realm. Even so, Satan came across as an adversary of God and a tempter, but subject to the powers of God. The point of the story to me is that God rewards faithfulness, and that his wisdom is far above that of mankind's. Man is to accept whatever happens without blaming God, for Satan is behind man's suffering.

Satan is described as the tempter of Jesus in three of the four gospels only John omits this story. Satan is described as having been given power over the earth and that he was able to confer some of that power to whomever would worship him. Again, Satan can only tempt, not force. Jesus answers all of Satan's temptations with scripture, and ultimately Satan backs off.

Is The Evil One Active Today?

Look around and see. Did God crash the planes into the twin towers? Did He cause the holocaust? Does He cause the untold murders and other crimes that we read about every day? I think not. Evil abounds in the world amidst the good that also occurs. Is there an Evil One at work in the world? I'm convinced there is. The nightly news and the morning papers shout it out. The Evil One whispers in my ear and wants me to be self-serving. He tempts, he distorts reality, but does not, and cannot, order or command. He just suggests, rationalizes, and paints a faulty picture of the truth.

Is the Evil One the cause of AIDS, small pox, the plague or a host of other natural disasters? I suspect not. God would not have allowed the Evil One to have power over nature. These natural disasters, I believe, are just the natural workings of nature.

The early prophets of the Hebrew Testament believed, to a man, that God was responsible for the punishments of the Israelite people. They warned the people that the punishments would come if the people continued to disobey God's covenant with them, and they did. While the logic is reasonable that God's chosen people, who disobeyed His commandments would bring corrective action by God, I don't understand that God would be quite so punitive, to bring death upon the just and the unjust. I see this as the action of the Evil One, and the natural consequence of sin.

Why is there an Evil One? I suspect, because as an angel among the heavenly host, he chose to challenge God's power and enter into conflict with Him. I must conclude then, that even in Heaven, God allows His children to retain choice in their relationship with Him. This is true in a marriage, couples retain their choice to remain married and keep and enrich their investment and commitment with their partner. I don't believe God made the Evil One as an evil being as it were, but allowed this particular angel's choice to occur and remain. God could have obliterated this angel gone wrong, but I believe because of God's love for all His creatures, even those gone wrong, He suffers with their recalcitrance. At least, this is what makes sense to me.

Mark, Matthew, and Luke all cite the temptation of Jesus by the Evil One. Mark gives one verse only, but Matthew gives the three main temptations, and this is virtually copied verbatim by Luke. How did the Evil One tempt Jesus? He did by offering to fulfill His needs when he was most vulnerable after a long period in the wilderness. Jesus responds to the Evil One, by citing to each temptation, the Hebrew laws given by God.

The scriptural setup was that Jesus was directed by the Spirit to go into the wilderness for a long period. During this time, He supposedly did not eat or possibly he survived on berries and water. The picture being painted was that Jesus would have been near starvation and his need for food would have been enormous. He should have been dead or near death had this been a real life scenario. In Jesus' case, the Evil One suggested that Jesus use His miraculous powers to transform stone into bread. Jesus countered with "Man shall not live by bread alone, but by every word that proceeds from the mouth of God." The lesson in this storyline of course is that man is tempted when he is most vulnerable, and that the temptation, which is most reasonable, is to take care of your own needs by whatever means possible. Jesus says that there is physical food, but what is more important is the spiritual food or wisdom that God provides.

I would speculate that the Evil One was after Jesus his entire life, but never made a dent. Jesus' spirit was firm and resolute, and he used His knowledge of God's laws to rebuke the Evil One every time. This is a model for us.

It is important for us to understand that there is an Evil One active in the world today fighting God by deceiving us into acts of selfishness and Evil. While the Evil One has the power of suggestion over us, we must recognize his existence and the tools of his trade to conquer him.

The Tools of the Evil One in today's Society

As we advance ever so slowly toward the Day of Judgment, I believe the Evil One is accelerating his efforts to recruit converts to himself. He must know his days are limited and he and his followers will be separated from the Eternal God forever. Regardless, we must be aware of his presence and the tools he uses to subdue people to his power. From a religious perspective, the tools that the Evil One uses to lead us astray are:

> Distorting the truth
> Offering Power and Position
> Manipulating Others
> Killing trust
> Losing perspective
> Blaming others
> Spreading fear
> Mistaking Priorities
> Generalizing and rationalizing

Distorting the Truth

We see in the current day a behavior of exaggerated rhetoric wherein language and meaning are twisted. For example, claims that health insurance reform are equated to "death squads deciding who should be refused end of life care and be sentenced to death" is exaggerated rhetoric. This is not real, but some Americans try to paint things with a fatal color.

"Enhanced interrogation techniques" is a euphemism and a distortion of the reality of torture of enemy combatants. American government and the military have violated both International and American law by torturing prisoners not yet found guilty of any crime in a court of law. There is nothing that justifies inhumane treatment of people we hold captive.

Government officials used to refer to hydrogen bombs, as "devices," as such it becomes euphemistic language that distorts truth. Similarly, when innocent civilians are killed in a war and we call this "collateral damage" we depersonalize people and hide the terrible tragedy of human suffering.

The Evil One distorted truth in the mythical Garden of Eden, and he continues to do so today. The writer of Genesis saw this and reported correctly. The Evil One promises wealth and power, but instead, destroys. Does anyone know a happy drug user?

Distortion of truth is the first step on the path to moral and national decay. How do we find truth in our society? We the people must demand it. First we must practice truth ourselves, and then teach our children the importance of being truthful. Finally, we must demand it from our media, our leaders, our advertising agencies, from those who preach to us, and from our fellow humans. Are we winning or losing on truth? While many see truth, those in power seem to distort it, so I think we are losing. We can do better.

The Bible proclaims the answer, "Seek the truth, and the truth shall make you free."

Offering Power and Position

The Evil One showed Jesus the kingdoms of the earth, or at least, what could be seen from a mountaintop. The offer was that the Evil One could put Jesus in charge of these kingdoms because he had the power to do so. The price was, that Jesus fall down and worship the Evil One. I suspect the price was delivered in fine print, or guarded whispers. Jesus responded with, "You shall serve the Lord your God, and Him only shall you serve." Jesus was making the point that there was one God, and only one God who shall be served. The culture of the period was that there were many Gods (at least among the Gentiles), but that the Hebrews had only one God.

The message I get from this transaction is that the Evil One has been given power (dominion over the earth). Where that power came from was omitted, but presumably from God. What was this power? It was only the ability to suggest. In all three temptation scenes, it was suggested to Jesus to:

Change the stones into bread
Take a leap of faith, you'll be rescued
Take the earthly power I can give you

The Evil One appeals to greed, our physical needs, and our wish to be cared for. He distorts reality, paints a rosy picture, denies the cost, rationalizes, and generalizes. He wants us to be disobedient to God. This happened in the Garden of Eden. The apple was described as an opportunity for wisdom and power. God's directive to refrain from eating the apple was downplayed and the Evil One rationalized that God wouldn't do anything harmful to Adam and Eve if they disobeyed His order.

The Evil One was quite silent about the fact that disobeying God brings about the natural consequence of pain and suffering. Is this God's fault, or that of the Evil One? I suggest the latter.

Manipulating others

In the gospel temptation stories the Evil One set Jesus at the top of the church spire, so to speak, and said, "Jump you won't get hurt, because the angels will take care of you." The Evil One was putting Jesus between himself and God, in an "I dare you situation." The Evil One was daring God, by using Jesus as a pawn. Jesus would have none of this, and responded to the temptation with the words, "You shall not tempt the Lord your God."

Jesus was in a precarious position, placed there by the Evil One, and the temptation was to ask God to get him out of this pickle. The message I get from this scene is that we should take responsibility to keep ourselves out a precarious positions, but if in one, don't manipulate anyone, including God, to get you out of it. Another way of saying this is, "Don't force God's Hand."

I was saddened when I heard some legislators saying they would vote for healthcare, but only if they could get multi-million dollar "earmarks" for their constituents written into the bill. This was a manipulation of the system. The fact that politics has always been this way doesn't change this manipulation from being an evil act.

Killing Trust

A marriage is a microcosm of a nation. Among the qualities that hold a marriage together, the most important is trust. When two people trust each other and become predictable in their behavior, then a marriage is stable. It does not rely on wealth or health. It relies on trust. When a trust is broken, then a marriage can crumble.

So it is in a nation. A nation is stable if there is trust between the people and its rulers. A nation must trust its political leaders. I find it unfortunate that some conservatives, at least, sew the seeds of mistrust in our government. It is as if they wish the government would fail, so that they could becomes the heroic rescuers of the very institution they would destroy. Such people who sew mistrust are doing the work of the Evil One.

Bernie Madoff betrayed the trust of those who gave him money to invest on their behalf. Those who cheat Medicare and Medicaid with illegal scams are in fact stealing from individual taxpayers. They are tearing down the very institution that protects them and provides services for them. Society functions only as long as there is trust between individuals and institutions.

We would live in chaos if we couldn't trust sellers to be honest. Similarly, we must trust insurance carriers to pay policyholders for damages to body and property according to contract provisions in the policy. There should be no hidden clauses in fine print that policyholders could not read or understand. Business must uphold the standards of integrity. Bottom line profits must never come before serving the customer honestly.

Iraqis learned that they could not trust Saddam Hussein, their leader, because he ruled not by consensus, but by fear. A citizen could never disagree with a policy put forth by the dictator; otherwise they could be jailed, tortured, or killed. Neighbors were recruited to spy on other neighbors, just like Hitler did in WWII. Neither Germans nor Iraqis could trust their neighbor, because they didn't know who was a spy. This kind of living was hell. We say, it could not happen here. Hopefully not, but the Germans and Iraqis lived that way only because they capitulated to individuals whom they saw as a potential heroes.

Stop reading and think for a minute how you would feel if you couldn't trust your neighbors, your government, or any institution you did business with. It would be hell. Therefore, we must protect trust and integrity with all our might.

Losing Perspective

In Chapter One I told the story of a mythical pope who concluded from his position in the papal garden that the sun revolved around the earth. He developed this conclusion from one viewpoint. Because he saw the skies only from one viewpoint, he had no perspective, and his conclusion was wrong. So it is in our culture.

Our legislators argue from a single point of view and fail to see a complete picture. Politicians are prone to argue from old paradigms that may not have value. Lowering taxes during the Bush administration did nothing to increase employment. It did little to help the poor, and it only widened the disparity of wealth in America. So we as a nation must challenge old paradigms that didn't work in the past. We must refocus our perspective and see multiple sides of a problem. It is right to argue, but those who do, must be open to other viewpoints. We as a people must also draw conclusions and argue only after looking at things from more than one viewpoint.

Corporations, in their effort to lower costs and improve profits have shipped jobs offshore where labor costs are lower. This may be reasonable from a cost view, but in so doing they have damaged our own middle class and their ability to purchase the very goods we manufacture. Consider the Romans. They had slave labor to build coliseums, temples, monuments and roads. As a result they had no middle class to purchase goods or to pay taxes. Free labor helped ruin their economy.

We tend to idolize beauty in our culture, particularly in women. We manufacture products and design clothing to enhance beauty. We can whiten teeth and remove wrinkles. Beauty, however, is a fleeting quality. On the outside it lasts just a few decades at most. Beautiful people can be vain, selfish or spiteful. Beauty is on the inside not the outside. It is the personality, attitude and behavior of people that make them beautiful. It is the love that people give that makes them beautiful, not the clothes they wear. When we focus on physical beauty and ignore true internal beauty, we have lost perspective on what is important in society.

Blaming Others

In the Genesis creation story, Adam blamed Eve, and Eve blamed the serpent, when God confronted them about their nakedness. They didn't own up to their betrayal of God's trust. Each played the role of victim.

Adolph Hitler pounced on this device to win the support of the German people. Germany was in a period of hard economic times, so Hitler portrayed the Germans as victims of the Jews. The Jews were just as economically depressed as anyone else, but he gave the people someone to blame and hate. By this ruse he rose to power.

We were all devastated by 9/11 and as soon as we learned that the perpetrators were extremist Muslims, we mentally placed all Muslims in any "enemy" position. First, doing this was a grand mistake of generalization. Second, instead of focusing on whom to blame, we might have asked the question, "Why did someone want to do this?" What did someone like Osama bin Laden, and/or others see in the United States that angered them to want to kill Americans. Was it our economic power, or smugness, or hypocrisy that caused this?

It could have been any of these or more, but their actions weren't appropriate. The perpetrators determined that they were victims of the American economic system, and that we were then the "enemy." We were the infidels, and they had the right to kill us. Now this was taking Scripture (the Koran) totally out of context.

The response of most Americans was first to stand beside our Muslim brothers and not let generalization lead us to equally inappropriate actions. Second, we still need to look at why some nations may disapprove of our behavior in the world and clean our own house. While Saddam Hussein may have been a dictator, and run roughshod over many of his people, there was no evidence that he had anything to do with 9/11. Our government chose to vindicate itself by retaliating against a reasonable enemy of our own making. I suspect those in power felt they could not find Bin Laden, so they honed in on an alternate visible target. This was a mistake, and many of us know it. We may have liberated a section of the Iraqi population, but we have also given many extremist Iraqis a reason to hate us.

Spreading Fear

Fear is another weapon of the Evil One. People faced with fear react with a self-preservation mode. Political strategists know this and exploit it to their advantage. Politicians against progressive change have typically used fear to defeat Congressional health bills proposing that a change would lead to catastrophe. This has caused voters to lose sight of the issues and vote instead on fear-based emotions.

Fear was used as a motivator to get the American people to support the Iraq war. The notion that terrorists were ready to pounce on America with nuclear and biological weapons required that we stop them in their own county. This was the message, and obviously people would respond to this logic. The fallacy was that terrorists had no nuclear or biological weapons and were not a threat to us.

Even as I write, the former Vice President continues to criticize the Obama Administration as "being soft on terrorism" and not understanding the threats. The Vice President gives no facts, only allegations. Presumably, his object is to raise fears among the people and get them to change their political affiliation.

Joseph McCarthy[1], Senator from Wisconsin (1947-1957), needed a major issue to bolster his run in the Senate for a second term in 1952. He chose to assert that 57 known Communist sympathizers had infiltrated the State Department and that he had a list of their names. In various speeches, he referred to 57, 81 and 205 Communists, in the Department although he never substantiated his claims.

He used his position as Chairman of the Committee on Government Operations and its Permanent Subcommittee on Investigations as his platform from which to accuse members of the State Department, the

Army, the entertainment industry, and even two presidents of either being Communists or traitors. He convinced his colleagues in Congress through fear that they had to purge its ranks of any and all suspected Communists. McCarthy used allegations, all unproven and innuendo to ruin the careers of many people. In hindsight, this turned out to be a horrendous miscarriage of justice. Over time, his unseemly and aggressive tactics were seen for what they were: demagoguery, witch hunting, and slander. The Senate ultimately censured him and he lost face in the nation.

The scary part of this history is that a great part of the American populace supported McCarthy based on the fears he generated. His appeal seemed reasonable, but only after it led to extremes and paranoia did his fellow senators realize that what he was doing was not helping the country. Likewise, the German people in the late 1930's fell for the fears that Adolph Hitler preached. They didn't question him. He gave them an enemy to blame for their troubles. The people paid dearly for their mistake during World War II.

In 2009 the American people are hearing fear rhetoric also. Many may fall in line and respond erratically. Americans must learn that they must separate fact from rhetoric. Only then can the country act responsibly.

Mistaken Priorities

I'd like to compare the priorities of the colonists of the 17th and 18th centuries with those priorities we have today. My ancestors came to Boston in 1636. Boston at the time had fewer than 3,000 residents, many of whom were Native American Indians. My forebears had to think carefully about what they brought on the wooden sailing ship that carried them for eight weeks across the Atlantic. They brought a horse or two, and a cow or two, and a few sheep. They had to bring enough hay and food for the animals to eat on the trip. They brought the tools to build a house, along with a few pieces of furniture. They brought some cooking and eating utensils and then just enough clothing to get them by. Finally they brought enough food to feed two adults and four children for eight weeks. Lucky they were if they could catch a fish along the way.

There were no Holiday Inns when they arrived. Probably they bunked in with friends who had preceded them to the new land. Their first task was to buy land, build a house and start a garden. They had to collaborate with their neighbors and with the Indians who were here long before them. There was no electricity, no televisions, and no golf courses in 1636, only hard work. The children all worked and helped their "pa" build the house and the barn. They built fences and they tilled the land. They dug a well and built an outhouse.

The pioneers struggled with the cold, fought with the few marauding tribes, and did their best to feed themselves on the rocky and rugged New England soil. There were many stones to move as the New England stone fences show.

This was early America, built with sweat and tears. The pioneers brought with them English Law, Protestant religion, and strong values. Among these values were religious liberty, equality among people, and adherence to the law.

Their priorities, as I see them were to:
- Sustain themselves
- Work together as a community
- Practice their religion in freedom
- Protect their system of law
- Fight for their independence a century later

From the perspective of financial backers in England, what was expected from the pioneers were repayment of loans and payment of profits. In 1765 taxes were exacted on all imported goods from the homeland. This caused a ruckus among the colonials and the taxes were lifted for a year or two, but re-imposed in 1767. This caused the great Boston Tea Party raid on the ships bringing tea to Boston. From this act was borne the phrase, "No taxes without representation."

Hard work and struggle were the hallmarks of early America. The fight for independence highlighted the 18th century. The birth of industry, the push westward, and the battle of conscience highlight the 19th century. The 20th century was about patriotism and war. We helped Europe stop German aggression twice and we fought in Asia twice to stop the spread of Communism and dictatorship rule.

Economic expansion took place in the 20th century and the disparity of wealth started to grow. Home ownership grew for the middle class. Church attendance became fashionable after World War II during the Eisenhower years. Television was born, air travel blossomed, and manufacturing grew, as did the automotive field.

Social change took place in the 20th century. Civil rights became a reality, at least for some, and college became possible for many servicemen through the GI Bill. Women entered the work force in WW II, and that trend continued to expand after the war. With television, the interest in sports mushroomed. The changes in the 20th century came so fast and in such quantity that it was mind-boggling.

Now in the 21st century some things changed and other trends expanded. Civil rights were slowly extended to Gays and Lesbians for the first time. This has taken place against a backdrop of conservative resistance even as did the rights of blacks 40 years earlier. Women began to be accepted into the world owned by men. Women now play in symphony orchestras and own businesses. Women's sports teams were organized and funded in public schools, colleges, and at the professional level. Women also rose in the corporate world and were accepted into public office at all levels.

Today our society has developed some paradigms that are not in its best interests. I list a few for example:

- "Money wins"
- "Twist the truth and you will win"
- "Guns will make us safer"
- "Individual rights exceed community rights"
- " It's okay to cheat, everybody does it"
- "If he's homeless, it's his fault"

Money wins, seems to be the story in baseball, for example. The Yankees win the World Series, because they buy the best players and consequently have the only $200 million-plus payroll in baseball. The playoff teams have payrolls in the $100 million category and the "also-rans" generally pay less than $100 million for their teams. This takes us to ask, "Why go through the baseball season?" If the owners could sit around a table and lay out their payrolls, then the two teams with the highest payrolls could go directly to the World Series without playing the season.

Politics is also a "money wins" institution. The acceptance of special interest money and the increasing demand for money from individual supporters has reached new heights. Money buys votes and special favors from Congress. Political demands for money are spiraling upward faster than healthcare costs, and are about out of control. That was never intended in 1776. Americans can have a better system.

Guns and Safety

Americans with guns kill over 12,000 people each year. Our society seems to accept the deaths of 33 Americans a day from guns. The tragedy at Columbine High School where two teenagers killed 13 others with guns before they turned the guns on themselves is a sign of a sick society. These boys may have felt as outcasts, but with guns they saw themselves as powerful.

Let me share one example of our badly prioritized values. Society puts up with 12,000 people being killed with guns and more thousands wounded thereby. Yet, when the Three Mile Island Nuclear plant had an accident wherein no one was killed or injured, an entire industry was shut down. Had the operator kept his hands in his pocket and just watched the plant instruments, the plant would have shut itself down quite safely as it was designed. The accident occurred because the operator overrode the safety systems. Even though the reactor was destroyed by the meltdown, little, if any, radiation was released because the containment building functioned as designed.

The industry was shut down because this single event touched off mass hysteria and fear that thousands could have died from cancer.

Perhaps if the 12,000 Americans that were killed with guns were all shot on the same day at the same time, maybe there would have been some mass hysteria that would have shut down the gun industry. Certainly on September 11th when 3,000 people were killed by terrorists there was a mass reaction. A Homeland Security

Department was created, virtually overnight. Plans for retaliation were started. Ultimately, a war was started.

Somehow when only 33 people are killed per day with guns, it doesn't seem to be a big deal. Perhaps it is profit that rules, or maybe individual rights to tote guns. Obviously, farmers and hunters have a need to have guns, but the rank and file doesn't need them. Self-protection is not a good reason. Teenagers above all, have no reason to own or get their hands on weapons. Whatever the reason, it doesn't make sense that we tolerate gun violence, but shut down a nuclear industry that was safe and didn't kill anyone. This is an example of misplaced priorities.

The gun industry has taken the Second Amendment to the Constitution too far, and out of context. Of course the patriots in 1775 needed weapons to defend their freedom against the British. They also needed guns to protect themselves against some marauding Indian tribes in New England back in the 17th century. That was the context for the second Amendment.

There is a right to own a gun, but why is there such a need? If our citizens feel they need protection, then there is something wrong with our society. If society feels it needs protection, then we must find out why, and solve that problem. It may be because of a power imbalance, which again ties to wealth disparity. Guns give power to the powerless, but more guns is not the solution.

Do you think there will be guns in Heaven if you get there? Will Jesus be packing a sidearm? Do you think you would be safer if everyone in America is issued a weapon? I suspect it is safer to be in Afghanistan than America, even when they have a power struggle going on. We don't lose thirty-three soldiers a day. We would quit if we did.

Individual Rights Exceed Community Rights

Gun ownership, in a sense, is an example of individual rights exceeding community rights. Being awarded unnecessarily high compensation versus allowing people to be homeless is another example. Today some are arguing that legalizing marijuana is a person's right, but then what about the community's right to have users under the influence off the streets? The Evil One uses deception again as his tool to make society unstable through the improper prioritization of rights.

It's Okay to Cheat Everybody Does It

This is an example of both generalization and rationalization. First, everybody does not cheat. The vast majority of people are honest and never cheat. A few do cheat and make it difficult for those that don't. Drug dealing and defrauding the government are two prevalent examples of cheating. To validate the practice by saying, "Everybody does it" is rationalizing. This is a tool of evil that we must be aware of and confront.

If He's Homeless it's His Fault

This is an example of shunning responsibility. The statement reminds me of God asking Cain, "Where is your brother, Abel?" The answer, "I don't know. Am I my brother's keeper" is an example of shunning responsibility. We, as a society, are responsible for each other. Society cannot exist as a group of individuals caring only for themselves without regard to their neighbors. That would be chaos. Yet, this argument is used by the Evil One constantly to promote disobedience to God. It is another way he deceives us, by inferring that we are not responsible for our neighbors. Jesus, himself, said in the second of the two greatest laws, "Love your neighbor as yourself."

You might form a different set of paradigms than I did, but the point I make is that the Evil One has a set of tools he uses to deceive people. The objective of the Evil One is to get people to follow him so that he might have power. We as individuals must not be deceived and we must prevent our society from being trapped by the Evil One. He does not give life he destroys it.

A Look at Adolph Hitler

Hitler came to power by using a prime tool of the Evil One, which was fear. The Germans were economically depressed and things were bad. Hitler said things could get worse, but he promised that he could fix things. He first found a group to blame for the country's economic woes – the Jews. Fear and blame were his first two tools, then he added a third, distortion of the facts. He changed the reality for the German people so they would buy into his promises of returned glory.

There were good times for the people for a while, until the price had to be paid. They were devastated by the war. The Evil One had played into Hitler's ego and sense of greed, and the rest is history.

The Jews paid for Hitler's sin and the Evil One's temptations. God did not punish the Jews, the Evil One used them as scapegoats. So it is with evil. The Evil One, appealing to the greed of mankind and submission to disobey God's advice and counsel, brings grief and death.

Will this go on forever? No, I think God will rein in the Evil One and isolate him and his adherents forever. Those who have chosen evil ways will be condemned to live with the fallen angel in isolation of God for eternity. That is my sense of Hell. It will not be a place of fire and brimstone, but of cold, dark isolation from the Love of God. That, to me, would be "Hell."

I suspect that the punishment of the Evil One will come from those he deceived. They will hate and despise him forever.

FOOTNOTE

[1] Wikipedia, *Joseph McCarthy*

CHAPTER 4

THE EVOLUTION OF THE
HEBREW CANON

One must not read the scriptures from the bottom rung
of the ladder of generality
There one will be caught up in the myths and legends
of ancient scriptural writers,
One must read from the top rung where the messages of the
Scriptures more easily will be found.

The Development of the Hebrew Bible

I imagine the authors of the first five books of the Hebrew Bible to be like painters or perhaps playwrights. They intended to draw pictures of what they believed to be God's interaction with His people. As playwrights, they were creating a narrative of the significant events in the lives of the Israelite tribes. Genesis first opens with the introduction of some key characters.

- The creation myth with God as the key player
- Adam and Eve enter second, representing the human race
- The Evil One follows as the villain

The points in the first three chapters of Genesis are:
1. God felt His creation was good
2. Mankind was imbued with God's own spirit
3. God walked with human kind and interacted with it
4. There was evil and deception from the very beginning
5. Humankind disobeyed God, and became separated from Him

Two points will be repeated many times in the Hebrew Canon:
- God directly acts with a single individual to guide His people
- The Hebrews believed that God punishes disobedience

Noah

We see next that God was upset with the violence and evil in the world and vowed to destroy it. God recognized Noah as righteous so

He directed him to build an ark and make room for as many species of animals as he could. Through all this Noah was obedient. The rains came and civilization as it existed was wiped out (at least in that part of the world.) The term "forty days" was not used as a precise duration. It meant "an extended period." Similarly, the term "three days" as in Jesus entombment meant "a short period," and not necessarily a precise number of days.

The Noah flood story was obviously an embellishment of a local flood. If it rained at a rate of 3 inches per hour (6 feet per day) there would only have been 280 feet of water after the 40 days. For the waters to have covered, say 19,000 ft high mountains, it would have had to rain almost 9 years steady. Noah's food supply in the ark would have long since been devoured. Suffice to say, that this story line is a mammoth extrapolation of a significant, but much smaller event. This might be considered the first of God's nature miracles.

When the flood subsided and Noah and his family could leave the ark, he built an altar and sacrificed clean animals to God. This act pleased God, and He promised Noah that He would not cause a similar event to happen again, and gave the rainbow as a seal of this promise.

The sacrifice of clean animals had obviously been carried out since prehistoric times, both in the Middle East as well as other parts of the world. This was the means by which mankind felt it could please God.

Abraham

Abraham was next on the scene. God promised that he would be the father of many nations. Since he and wife Sarah were past the change of life period, this promise seemed just short of being ludicrous. God said, to wait and see, that nothing was too hard for the Lord. Now previously, Sarah had given her servant Hagar to Abraham for sexual relations, and she bore a son Ishmael. He was to be the father of the Islamic world. Sure enough Sarah had a son, Isaac, who was to be the progenitor of the Hebrew nation. The story continues when Abraham is asked to sacrifice Isaac. This is a strange test of faith. How could God promise Abraham one thing, and then immediately ask him to give up that which was given him? To my knowledge, the people of the Middle East did not practice human sacrifice, but only animal sacrifice (there could have been pagan exceptions to this). The sacrifices were burned so the odors would rise into the sky to be noticed by God. Abraham proceeded with blind obedience in the story, and was rescued at the moment of the sacrifice when a ram was provided, caught in a bush. Consider the Isaac story when comparing it to the story of Jesus as a human sacrifice.

A side story about Abraham was his prolonged negotiation with God about the fate of those people in Sodom who were righteous. The negotiation was as if two men were arguing a business deal. In this case Abraham seemed to be winning his argument that God should not destroy an entire city if there were some good people living there. Why penalize the good along with bad? Abraham argued God from fifty good people down to five. Then God told Abraham to get those five good people out of town, He was going to punish evil. So the volcano erupted or the earthquake came and the town was destroyed. The last bit of disobedience occurred when Lot's wife looked back on the desolation, and she was supposedly turned into a pillar of salt.

What are the key messages with the Abraham story?

- Blind obedience is rewarded
- The faithful are tested to see if they really trust God
- God will ultimately destroy evil
- God will listen to a righteous man and hear his arguments
- We hear the first miraculous birth story

God Makes Good Results Out Of Bad Happenings

The Hebrew narrative turns to the eleventh son of Jacob; Joseph. Jacob apparently favored young Joseph and in token, gave him a coat of many bright colors. This made the older ten brothers jealous. They conspired to kill him, but Reuben convinced the others to put Joseph into a pit where he might starve to death. Reuben had in mind to secretly rescue Joseph later.

It turned out that a caravan came by heading south to Egypt, and rather than letting Joseph die, they sold him for 20 shekels of silver. The reader might remember this betrayal for money, for it will be recalled in the New Testament. Joseph was a bright young fellow and early on had a reputation for being able to interpret dreams, which further irritated the older brothers. Joseph was sold to one of Pharaoh's officers, and he did well, but because he was handsome and intelligent his master's wife tried to seduce him. He would have none of that, so she falsely accused him of attempted rape and he was jailed for two years or more before Pharaoh had a disturbing dream that begged for interpretation. The rest you know. Joseph rescued Egypt from famine and he was the instrument by which the Hebrew people moved into Egypt to escape the area-wide famine in Judea.

The Genesis author showed that God took a bad happening to innocent Joseph and turned it into a life-saving event for the twelve tribes of Jacob (Israel). Joseph was reconciled to his brothers. His father, Jacob, was ecstatic to see his son alive and well, and they were all given land in Egypt to plant and graze their animals.

Good Things Come To An End

After Joseph died, the Hebrew people had multiplied and became a large bloc of people. Because of this, subsequent Pharaohs saw the Hebrews as a nuisance and a security threat, but also a source of slave labor. The Hebrews were forced to build store-cities and monuments to the Pharaohs. In spite of the 400 years of oppression, Abraham's people continued to grow in numbers, causing the Pharaoh (probably Rameses II) to order his troops to drown in the Nile every young male Hebrew baby they could find. Rameses wanted to end the growth of the Hebrew population.

During this period Moses was born, found by Pharaoh's daughter, and raised as an Egyptian. The story of Moses is well known. He was appointed by God to rescue the Hebrew people from bondage and to be their lawgiver.

Moses was perhaps Israel's mightiest hero. He had a sense of justice, and was quick to defend a Hebrew woman who was being cruelly beaten by an Egyptian taskmaster. He killed the Egyptian and buried him, which quickly lead to his defection from the house of Pharaoh. When called by God to lead his people out of Egypt, Moses had many excuses to rebut God. God would not be talked out of His decision, but did offer brother Aaron to be the spokesperson for Moses.

Moses confronted Rameses with the demand to "let his people go." There followed nine plagues upon the land that finally wore Rameses down to the point of admitting that Moses' God was more powerful than the Egyptian gods, however he wouldn't budge on letting the people go.

The tenth plague would follow, but only after the Hebrews were instructed to prepare for what was to become the Passover rite that would save their first-born children from death by the imminent plague. The deaths of the Egyptian children, including Pharaoh's own, convinced Pharaoh to let the Hebrews take whatever spoils they could carry and then leave.

Next came the Red Sea adventure, the rescue by God, and the extended journey toward the Promised Land. Scholars discount the size of the Exodus of 600,000 men plus women and children. It may be more reasonable to assume the group was about 250,000 total. This is a huge logistical nightmare when considering how to feed all these people and their animals on a long and arduous journey.

The Hebrew Testament playwrights were careful to note that God provided for their sustenance, one day at a time, with manna from heaven (so to speak). He was continually asking them to trust. In ancient understanding, God was to have descended from the sky to mountaintops where only the elect mediators like Moses could ascend and meet privately with God. Moses left Aaron in charge of the people while he and Joshua ascended Mount Sinai to hear God's instructions. Moses had Joshua wait for him part way up, while he went farther. There he encountered the burning bush, and was given the Ten Commandments etched in stone. In addition he was instructed to build the Ark of the Covenant and the Tent of Meeting, plus other instructions on providing priestly robes for Aaron as the chief priest of the people. The writer cites that Moses was atop the mountain for many days. While there, God indicated that He knew the Hebrew people had lapsed into idolatry and He was in a rage to blot them out. Moses argued with God like Abraham before him, to abate His anger until he could find out what was going on and restore order.

Moses found Joshua and they returned to find the people reveling about a golden calf they influenced Aaron to make for them. Aaron offered Moses some lame excuses for his miscreant actions, and Moses, in a fit of anger, smashed the tablets of stone, and had the golden calf melted, then ground down to powder, and then mixed with water. As a final gesture of anger, he made the people drink the water. The temperment of the Hebrews changed, for Moses made them understand they had displeased God. They looked to Moses to atone for them. Moses went back up Mt. Sinai and came back with a second set of Commandments to be placed in the Ark of the Covenant.

The biblical scriptwriters were quick to show that God inflicted a plague upon the people to remind them that sin is punished.

A concept to raise here is the ancient belief that blood sacrifices were efficacious for the atonement of sin. Since blood was the essence of life, sacrificing blood was an exchange of a sinning life for a new life, in the traditions prevalent at the time. The ancient sacrifices were seen as a substitution of the animal for the person offering the sacrifice. The animal was the atonement for the sin of the human. The animals had to be male and perfect in every respect. This may also have been a pagan understanding as well.

The Israelites wandered in the wilderness for forty years (a generation, or a long time). During this period the Hebrews developed many laws concerning religious and civil behavior. The Levites were designated to be the priestly class. The Israelites developed their pattern of worship, and they became unique in that they worshipped a single God.

Moses had to have been a devout man, but with a fierce temper, yet with courage and conviction. He felt the burden of being responsible for directing his people for forty years and getting them organized and fed, and keeping them in line. Moses, like Abraham, offered blind obedience to God. Moses saw the Promised Land, but never entered it. That role was left to Joshua. It is alleged that Moses was not allowed to enter the Promised Land because God was punishing him for murdering the Egyptian taskmaster.

The Book of Numbers relates that a census was taken from the various tribes so that an army could be raised proportionately from each tribe except the Levites. The army would be necessary as the Hebrews advanced into territory that they would have to fight for.

Israel Consolidates as a Kingdom

Joshua and his army conquered most, but not all, of the Promised Land. He apportioned the land gained to the various tribes. The Israelites did battle with the Philistines to the west, but were defeated. In a second battle, the Hebrews were completely overwhelmed and actually lost the Ark of the Covenant who placed it in a temple adjacent to the pagan god Dagon. Legend has it that the statue of Dagon fell to the ground twice before breaking apart the second time, when the Philistines decided the Ark was too dangerous to keep. The Ark was moved to various towns and each was stricken by a plague. Finally, the Philistines pleaded with the Israelites to take the Ark back. The message there was that God would not tolerate being placed among other false deities.

Samuel came on the scene in the role of a national judge, and ultimately the people demanded that a king be appointed to lead them as a nation. Saul was the first king followed by David, and then his son Solomon. While king, Saul spent most of his time in battle with the Philistines and the Amalekites. He was told by God to utterly destroy those with whom he came in conflict and to give no quarter to men, women, children, and animals. The purpose to commit genocide against Israel's enemies was to remove any source of competitive idol worship as a stumbling block for the Israelites. This seems ruthless to us in the 21st century, but the history of the Middle East is one of consistent and ruthless "Holy Wars," a term that has reappeared among Muslim extremists today.

Saul spared the life of Agag, king of the Amalekites, and took the Amalekite animals as spoils. God seemed to speak only to Samuel, and not to Saul, and He said that He repented ever having made Saul King of Israel, because he did not follow His commandments. Saul had prepared a sacrifice of the Amalekite animals to God, but God replied through Samuel, that he wanted obedience, not sacrifice.

Saul ultimately personally killed King Agag, but was soon thereafter mortally wounded and defeated in battle with the Philistines, as were his sons. Rather than be slain by the Philistines, Saul fell on his own sword.

Before Saul died, Samuel was directed by God to go to Bethlehem and interview the sons of Jesse, from whom God would choose His next leader. Samuel interviewed the first four sons, and clearly saw that none of these was to be God's elect. Inquiring whether there were any other sons, Jesse said his youngest was tending their flocks in the fields. Samuel asked Jesse to have him fetched, and when he arrived, Samuel knew that David was the chosen one.

David was personable, intelligent and a strong leader. When he became the king he was faithful to his God, yet he was an adulterer and a murderer. He coveted Uriah's wife, Bathsheba, and arranged to have Uriah killed in battle, so that he could have Bathsheba. So it is with Israel's heroes, they seem to fall short of the Glory of God, yet He still uses them to draw the Israelite people to Himself. David paid the price for his sin, by losing the very son that Bathsheba first bore to him, Absolom.

David's second son, Solomon, was to follow him as King of a united Israel. Solomon prayed for, and was granted, wisdom by God because his wish was not selfish, but for a capability to rule over his people. Solomon of course, built the first temple in Jerusalem. He used conscripted labor, but not slave labor, to build his opulent headquarters and worship center in Jerusalem. David had warned Solomon that he must follow the laws of Moses lest his kingdom fall into ruin. This he did until he reached the zenith of his power, then by marrying foreign women who were polytheistic, he fell into polytheistic worship. As predicted, this caused the downfall of Israel and Solomon's kingdom.

The United Kingdom divided into a northern kingdom (Israel), and a southern kingdom (Judah). The two kingdoms sparred with each other, and held an uneasy existence together. Tribal jealousies were still the order of the day. Israel was the first kingdom to fall, then to the Assyrians about 722 B.C.E. A multitude of Israelites were deported to Babylon and their properties in Israel were taken over by the conquering Babylonians.

The Babylonians conquered Judah in 586 B.C.E. and Jerusalem and its temple were destroyed. Again, more Israelites were deported into Babylon. In 538 B.C.E. Cyrus, King of Persia overthrew the Babylonians, and by edict, the Israelite captives were given their freedom to return to Israel and Judah. Many returned, but a number stayed since they had acquired positions of stability and wealth where they were. The second temple was rebuilt in Jerusalem by 515 B.C.E.

Next came Alexander the Great to conquer the area and spread Greek culture among the peoples. The Ptolemies of Egypt ruled the Jews primarily until the Romans conquered the area about 60 years before Jesus was born.

A Summary of the Hebrew History

We can probably estimate that the history of the Semite people of whom Abraham was the first Patriarch began about 1770 B.C.E. The people were semi-nomadic, following their herds to various grazing lands up to the mountains and back down to the plains. They had to have been a tent people, picking up their scant belongings whenever it was time to seek out a new pasture.

The people were polytheistic, worshiping various gods whom they believed exercised power over food, fertility, health, etc. The people organized themselves by clans and tribes for self-protection. Noah may have preceded Abraham by some centuries, so it could be the history of the Hebrew people may have started about 2,000 years B.C.E. or before.

During this period, the people spent about 400 years in Egypt where they were treated well as the people of Joseph during famine years. Later they became a threat and became slave labor. Moses rescued the people about 1225 – 1200 B.C.E. and took them to Mt. Sinai where they received the law from God. There, the covenant was established that they should worship only the one true God, and in return they would be given the land of Palestine. While in the southern wilderness, they established the Judaic form of worship and appointed themselves a priestly class from the tribe of Levi, and built an army from among the remaining tribes of Jacob. Between 1028 B.C.E. and 933 B.C.E. the twelve tribes of Israel had established a united kingdom, which was ruled by Kings Saul, David, and his son Solomon.

Petty jealousies among the twelve tribes ruined a good thing. They had a strong unified kingdom and it reached the heights of power and opulence under Solomon. When Solomon started pursuing the gods of his many foreign wives, the unified religion of the Hebrews started to unravel. Israel, the northern kingdom, would not pay taxes to, nor serve under Solomon's son Rehoboam, so they seceded and elected their own kings. The northern kingdom lasted about 211 years (933 B.C.E. – 722 B.C.E.) when the Assyrians overwhelmed them. By 705 B.C.E. Israel ceased to exist and over 27,000 Israelis were exiled to Babylon.

Judah, the southern kingdom fell to King Nebuchadrezzar of Babylon in 605 B.C.E. and by 586, it also ceased to exist. More Israelis went into exile. The land promised, and given by God was snatched away. The Hebrews had not kept their end of the covenant, and because of their apostasy, God let them suffer the consequences.

For the next 900 years, the land of Israel was occupied and ruled by the following:
  Babylonians (586 – 538)
  Persians   (538 – 332)
  Alexander   (332 – 323)
  Ptolemies   (323 – 198)
  Seleucids   (198 – 168)

The Maccabees liberated the Jews and they were free for 105 years (168 – 63), but then they fell under the rule of the Roman Empire (63 B.C.E. – 325 C.E.)

The Context of the Hebrew Canon

The Hebrew Testament was written over a thousand year period approx. (1150 B.C.E. – 130 B.C.E.). The Pentateuch was finished about 400 B.C.E. Much of the Hebrew history was passed between generations orally before it was ever written down. By the time Alexander the Great reigned and the Jews in Alexandria had written a Greek version of the Hebrew Testament and Apocrypha it was about 90 C.E. That's when the Hebrew Cannon was closed. Jesus had been born and had died, and the New Testament was being formed.

The Hebrew cannon was written against a backdrop of pain and turmoil. The people were driven to and fro in the hands of their enemies. However, they had their heroes. God spoke directly to the patriarchs; Abraham, Isaac, and Jacob and given a promise of their own land, if they but served the Lord God and Him only. The Hebrews did unite under Moses to swear allegiance to a monotheistic deity, but certainly wavered in that allegiance. They wrote of the many times God rescued them. They wrote about His presence among them while they were in the Wilderness, as a cloud of dust by day, and a pillar of fire by night.

God was their mighty hero who led them to military victories over the occupants of the Promised Land. He gave them civil laws to govern themselves, plus religious laws to govern their worship of Him. He strengthened the nations and gave them key leaders, judges, prophets, and kings to lead them. The prophets warned the people to mind their ways, but the kings, except David, seemed to fall into idolatry.

What is the Hebrew cannon as written by Hebrew people? It is a love story between God and a group of people He chose to worship Him. He walked and interacted with His selected leaders. He provided advice and counsel, and warnings. God tested His leaders, and wanted nothing short of blind obedience from them. The relationship He wanted had to be based on trust.

The Testament told of the actions of God, and those of the Israelite people. The history of the people is given in great detail. The laws and the religious rites were detailed. Psalms of praise were included and the wisdom of Solomon was also given. The history of the judges, kings and prophets were all written.

The picture of God in the Hebrew Testament was one:
- Who showed might and power
- Who performed miracles
- Who interacted with His people
- Who was jealous
- Who was ruthless to the heathen
- Who would listen to His leaders and was willing to negotiate with them
- Who provided for the needs of His people
- Who demanded obedience and trust

The early writers wrote miraculous deeds attributed to God and His leaders; Abraham, Moses, and Elijah. Jonah lived three days in the belly of a whale, it was said. A lightning bolt from heaven consumed the sacrifices of Elijah at the contest with the priests of Baal at Mt. Carmel. He also lifted Elijah into heaven on a fiery chariot while yet alive. The writers embellished to make a point.

The writers painted a picture of a mighty, powerful, and vengeful God who gave no quarter. The wars of the time were vicious and the innocent were slain as quickly as the warriors.

The Biblical writers also portrayed the people to be fickle, sometimes putting the Lord God first in their lives, then sliding backward into alien god worship. The writers showed their leaders to be heroes, but never failed to point out their sins.

The Canon Principles

Far be it for a non-Jewish layperson to explain the Hebrew Canon, I do it recognizing my inadequacies, but some basic principles are clear to me:
- The Hebrews believed that they alone, were chosen by God to be His people, separate and apart from the world at the time, to witness to God's glory.

- They separated themselves from the rest of the world by the rite of circumcision, by not intermarrying with others, and by adhering to very rigid rules of worship.

- They believed that God actively interacted with Hebrew leaders and with nature, to protect the Hebrews and bring them to the Promised Land.

- They saw God as one who punishes sin and disobedience.

- They felt that God was physically present with them, whether on the Mercy Seat on the Ark, or in the Holy of Holies, or in the burning bush, or in the Pillar of Fire. As God walked with Adam in the Garden, so He walked with them toward the new Promised Land.

- They believed in the atonement for sins with the sacrifice of unblemished, perfect male animals. The animals took the place of the donor. In this rite, the lamb was sacrificed, but the goat was heaped with the sins of the people and driven into the desert to die. This was the "scapegoat."

- The Hebrews saw God as almighty, all-powerful, jealous, and vengeful, yet faithful in His investment with His people. He was to be feared. It is interesting to note, that a reading of the Koran leaves a similar impression that God was to be feared above all else, and not to be taken lightly.

The only copies of the Hebrew Testament were kept in the Temples as scrolls. The Torah was read such that a reading was completed in exactly one year. That practice remains to the present. The other books were also read in Temple, but on a three-year cycle. The Temple was the place where the Hebrews learned the scriptures, but I'm sure they were verbally repeated in the tents of the faithful.

A key element of Hebrew theology was the shedding of blood for the atonement of sins. The blood could not be consumed, but was splashed around the altar, or sprinkled on the congregants so that they could be at "one-ness" with the sacrifice.

Good Jews were quite familiar with their history as told through oral tradition and the scriptures. They were familiar with their heroes. The writers of the scriptures had limited vocabulary, but they had the need to express their awe of God and their heroes with miraculous stories. Their purpose was to make an impact on the reader, and not to convey scientific facts.

In the next chapter we'll see what happened when God visited the Hebrews in the form of Jesus the Christ. We'll see that Jesus expanded the invitation to the Hebrews to be His people to the gentiles (the non-Jews).

CHAPTER 5

THE NEW VISIT FROM GOD

God will not let us go,
He will not be defeated by evil, but will conquer it,
However, neither will He take away our free choice.

How We Understand this New Visit

The Hebrew people felt God's presence with them, either in the pillar of Fire, through the prophets, or in other ways. God was real to them and he dwelt on earth. The Hebrews had many messengers from God. They were Noah, Abraham, Isaac, Jacob, Elijah, Moses, and David, just to name a few. These messengers had a number of things in common; they were devout and obedient, but none was perfect. Some of the adventures of these people were mythical, but the Hebrew Testament writers ascribed miraculous stories about these men because they represented God acting within the Hebrew people.

Jesus came to Israel and made such an impact that the New Testament writers also ascribed miraculous deeds to Him. This was consistent with the Jewish method of expression. We, in the modern western world, look at the facts, and then trip over them. We see a magical God who performed miracles in a scientific sense, but we miss the points that the writers were trying to make. The appearance of Jesus, in whom they saw God, in their time of occupation by the Romans, was indeed to them a miraculous event. What they expected to happen, the overthrow of the Romans, didn't happen. Jesus asked His people to change their focus from the Romans to God.

Forgetting for a moment the question of Jesus' divinity, the fact is that through Jesus, God came again to the people of the world offering us a renewed call to live in harmony with Him. This requires that we renounce sin and live consistent with God's perfection, as He intends us to do. To live in moral perfection is not for God's benefit, it is for ours. God knows that evil and sin will destroy us, but living unselfishly and in harmony with all of our brothers and sisters, and with God Himself, will give us boundless joy.

This time, the message of God, was not to be carried by one man delivered only to those in Judea and Galilee, but to be carried by the Apostles and delivered to the entire world. And so it happened that the message of God was in fact, spread widely by many and carried to the people in Africa, Asia, and Europe in the first millennium. Was that the last visit by God, possibly not? He has sent many people with specific roles to fulfill. Martin Luther was one to reform the church; Johann Sebastian Bach was another to bring glorious music to worship, Mother Theresa was to give aid and comfort to the poor, Martin Luther King Jr. was yet another to bring justice on behalf of an enslaved black population. These, and many others have had different missions and skills to bring to the tasks that God has asked them to do.

A Way to Understand our Relationship with God

I propose a very simplistic way to look at our relationship with God. It is an analogy, but it works for me. As I read the Koran, I was upset with Muhammad's portrayal of God as one to be mightily feared. I thought, "That's not the way that two people who love each other act. They relate to each other without fear." If Muhammad meant to "respect" God, I would understand. That is appropriate, particularly in a parent-child relationship. As children, we take for granted the wisdom, experience, and love our parents show us.

Consider this analogy. Our time on earth is like a courtship. The courtiers are we people and God. Like any couple that meet who have not known each other, there may or may not be an immediate attraction. If there is an attraction, there would follow a period of getting to know each other to find out if there are mutual likes, dislikes, goals, and dreams. All of this may derive from a selfish need to be wanted or to "have" someone to make us feel whole. The motive for the search for a partner may be selfish, or it may be to find someone who will receive our care giving and love.

The suitor will typically be outgoing and giving, at least in the beginning. A healthy relationship will be one of sharing and equality with a measure of giving and a measure of receiving. It. The goal will be to reach a pass-fail point beyond which is either a commitment or abandonment. In a good marriage there should always be a commitment to attend to the needs of the other partner and to help that partner live his or her life to the fullest.

Is this not what God wants for us? He wants us to be free from sin and selfishness and to be perfect like He is, so we can have a relationship as parent-child full of respect, admiration, and love. Do we create a commitment if we attend to our own selfish ways and ignore totally our partner or the one suited? Of course not. If we love God, as Jesus taught us, then we will do those things that please Him. We will have an attitude of respect for God, and will love Him by loving our neighbor and by reaching out to others. God gave us the ability to marry and to create children so we could experience the type of relationship He wants us to have with Him.

He always gives us the free choice to love Him or ignore Him. Free choice and trust are what give meaning to any relationship. Realize that He also retains the free choice to accept us or reject us. I don't accept predestination as an act of God to summarily dismiss any of us at His whim, but I do believe that God is under no obligation to accept us either. The freedom of choice works both ways. We are accepted into a relationship with Him partly as an act of our choice and acceptance, and always as an act of His grace.

Does this make sense to you? God does not wish a master-slave relationship with us. He wants a more nearly horizontal relationship. We will always have a parent-child relationship with Him as Jesus has a Father-Son relationship. If we can be perfect like Him, He can enjoy us, and we can enjoy Him. Will we ever be of the same substance as He? No, but we can be "like him." Our chief end, as the Westminster Catechism puts it, "Is to worship God and enjoy Him forever."

To me, achieving "salvation" as it were, is not the product of a ritualistic answer to a question, but it is demonstrating actions toward the one you love. It means attending to the best interests of your loved one. It involves attending worship and giving honor to God. It also means living out the teachings of Jesus. By loving our neighbors, we show that we love God. Further, as Jesus taught, it is loving our enemies, and those who would spitefully use us. As it was written, God said, paraphrasing scripture, "I'm not interested in your sacrifices, I'm interested in mercy and justice." God was saying that He was less interested in rituals than in acts of goodness, so that we all might enjoy the fullness of life.

The New Message from Jesus

God visited us in the person of Jesus, but what did He say?

The two most important teachings of Jesus were:
- To love God with all your might, mind and soul
- To love your neighbor as yourself

Jesus gave many parables, but the sum of what he was driving at was, "be like your heavenly Father." Treat others the way you wish others would treat you, and He implied: "Treat others like you would wish God would treat you on judgment day." We don't love God by reaching up into the sky, but rather by reaching outward to the least of his children, who need love and help.

We know by example, that we must take on the role of servant, and to be obedient even unto death. All of the prophets, although imperfect, were obedient. The New Testament indicates that none of the apostles put up an argument to Jesus' call. They followed Him without question. Again, I feel that obedience is asked for our good, not for God's. This is where faith comes in. If we can trust God, whom we cannot see, but are obedient to His wishes, then we will find eternal life.

Jesus raised the bar in terms of our attitudes and behavior towards others:

The old Mideastern custom was: "An eye for an eye."
    Jesus changed that to:
- Love your enemies,
- Show good to those who hate you
- Bless those that curse you
- Pray for those who abuse you

He went further to say:

- If someone slaps you on the cheek, turn to him the other cheek
- If someone takes your coat, offer him also your shirt
- If someone compels you to walk with them a mile, walk a second mile
- He said, don't find fault with your brother without first looking at your own faults
- He advised, "Be merciful as your heavenly father is merciful."

There is nothing that relates to liturgical legalism in what Jesus taught. He did not talk about sacrifice, other than it may have related to obedience. He only referred to himself as a sacrifice; He was using familiar terms and language that the Hebrews knew.

The Good News

The Good News as I see it was that God returned to earth through Jesus to give a message of hope to the poor and the marginalized. He was intervening to show them how they could live fulfilled lives even though living under Roman rule. God did not come to liberate the Jews from the Romans as the Jews had hoped, but to show them how they might live together in peace and how they might relate to non-Jews.

Jesus took the Jews out of their tribal mentality and showed them a higher standard of treating other people. Jesus swept away the attitude that the Jews would have no dealings with the Samaritans. He tore down the defensive walls that the Jews had put up to isolate themselves from other peoples. He opened their eyes to the reality of life after death.

Jesus was also to show that the life to come after death was to be a life of perfection, something better was coming, and those who choose to accept it, would be welcomed into God's family.

The Lost Sheep

Jesus indicated in his parable, that a good shepherd has his eye out for his entire flock (of 100) and if one sheep gets lost, he will leave the ninety-nine and go find the one that is lost. The message says that everyone is important; God will not lose a single person if He can prevent it. We must see in this parable the message that the Kingdom of God is inclusive, not exclusive.

The Apostles

When Jesus began his ministry, he asked twelve blue-collar workers to follow him and be his students. These folks were fishermen, farmers, tax collectors, and the like. There were no priests among them, or highly educated men. Peter and Andrew, James and John, Matthew and the others were ordinary people. It took them a while to understand who Jesus was. Peter was the first to grasp it. "You are the Christ, the Son of the Living God," said Peter. He saw God working through the carpenter's son. This understanding empowered these men to reach out to the world and preach the message of salvation.

The Jewish Temple hierarchy didn't get it. They felt their position of authority and importance was being threatened. They didn't comprehend his message. They did not see him as the Messiah because they had a pre-formed image of what the Messiah would do, that is, rid them of the Roman occupation. Therefore, they collaborated with the Romans to have Jesus silenced.

We didn't hear about all of the disciples after Jesus' death and resurrection, but some became leaders of the movement of Jesus. Matthew wrote a gospel. Peter became an evangelist among the Jews, wrote some epistles, and ultimately became a martyr in Rome. John, the son of Zebedee wrote a gospel, some letters, and at least some of the book of Revelation. James and Jude, half brothers of Jesus obviously were active in spreading the gospel of their brother. Some of their writings were included in the new Christian Canon.

The apostles did not take the church to their graves in the first century, rather they passed their roles on to others. Today, there are clergy and laypeople alike who are empowered by the Spirit, to continue to give messages of hope and encouragement to the marginalized and others in the shrinking world. If you are a layperson or clergyperson, don't for a moment assume you are not one of God's chosen apostles.

CHAPTER 6

THE EVOLUTION OF THE CHRISTIAN CANON

The early Christian scriptures were written primarily by Jews
for Jews and converts to a new and yet, unnamed religion.
The theology of the Hebrew nation became the backdrop for the
new Christian religion

Sources

As past Chair of the Lectureship committee of my church, I have been privileged to bring to Denver and talk with, and listen to, the lectures of Dr. Bart D. Ehrman, Professor of Religious Studies at the University of North Carolina, Bishop John Shelby Spong, Professor Marcus Borg, Dr. John Dominic Crossan, Rev. Dr. Peter Gomes, and Prof. Walter Bruggemann among others. I have also listened to the series of DVD lectures by Professor Amy Jill-Levine, Dr. Bart Ehrman, and Professor Phillip Cary, all of whom have been invaluable to me to more clearly understand the development of the Christian Testament.

Early Systems of Religion

Paganism

Paganism was a religion that was polytheistic, but with a minimal belief system. The gods were represented physically by carved idols, probably of wood or stone, and various gods represented power over some aspect of earthly existence such as fertility, the harvest, the sun, rain, or other factors that were essential to human survival. The belief system was simple; if we sacrifice to you, you will make things right for our survival. The pagans didn't have to believe anything about the gods. It was a straight deal; if you please us, we'll please you.

The action of the people was to sacrifice something of value, whether human, animal, or vegetable. Ethics played no part in this kind of worship. People did not have to be good to earn the favor of the gods, they just had to give something as an inducement to the gods to care for their needs and they could transfer their anxieties to the deity and wait for a change. Pagan religions that believed in an afterlife, did not conceive of it as an act of their gods, but of their own actions of sacrifice.

Hinduism and Buddhism

Hinduism and Buddhism and their various versions developed well before the Judeo-Christian eras. Hinduism is considered to be the oldest organized religion. It was not founded around any one heroic figure, but Hindus do believe in a single supreme deity. Buddhism, in contrast, is founded on the Buddha, Siddhartha Gautama. Buddhism evolved about 1,000 years after Hinduism, which was entrenched in India. Buddhism does not worship a deity, but seeks internal enlightenment to enable one to escape the cycles of reincarnation and to finally find Nirvana. Both religions have tended to be tolerant and peaceful. Hinduism unfortunately supports the caste system, and lowers the status of women.

The Hebrew Religion

The Jews believed in one true God who chose them uniquely to be His people. Through Moses, God gave them laws by which they should live and worship Him. The Ten Commandments were ethical laws by which the Hebrew social system could survive.

God also gave Moses the beginnings of the liturgical laws on Moses' second trip up Mount Sinai. After the tribe of Levi was selected to take on the priestly function dealing with liturgical laws such as; worship, circumcision, observance of the Sabbath, and of kosher food rules, among many others. Jewish author A.J. Jacobs cites in his book *The Year of Living Biblically* that medieval Rabbi Maimonides compiled a list of 613 rules he had found in the Pentateuch by which Orthodox Jews were to live. These laws are found predominantly in Exodus and Leviticus. Regardless of the precise number of laws, we can see that the Hebrew religion, particularly conservatives, could easily have become quite legalistic in their practice of religion. An example of this is found in Mark 3:23, when on the Sabbath Jesus' disciples plucked grain to eat while walking through the fields.

The Pharisees said this was unlawful, but Jesus pointed them to King David, who fed hungry men with the Bread of the Presence, which was legally set aside only for the priests to eat. Jesus was putting the needs of the people ahead of rigid observance of laws.

Like the pagans, Hebrews offered sacrifices; some of which were offered to God, and some to the Temple priests. They had very strict rules concerning the quality of sacrifices. The Jews believed that God was exclusively bonded to them and that eternal life, if any, was the result of their piety and devotion to the observance of the law.

Christianity

Christianity as expressed in the Pauline tradition, was based on a belief system about who Jesus was and what He did. Mankind's salvation was based on what God did rather than what people did. Salvation was achieved by believing that Jesus died in atonement for mankind's sin and that his resurrection represented that believers too would be resurrected. It was necessary that people believed that God's new covenant with all peoples was manifested in Jesus' death, burial, and resurrection.

Sacrifice per se, circumcision, and observance of the liturgical laws were not a part of Paul's theology. There was great debate whether gentiles had to subscribe to Jewish laws in order to be Christian. Those who held this view lost out and new followers of Christ were not obligated to follow Jewish traditions.

Christians further believed that the Hebrew Testament was really theirs, because of the fulfillment of the prophecies below. Matthew, in particular, wrote for a Jewish audience and took every possible opportunity to tie Hebrew canon writings into the life of Jesus to show that he was the long-expected Messiah.
    The prophetic writings:

Jesus would be born	In accordance with Scripture	Isaiah 7:14
Jesus would suffer	In accordance with Scripture	Psalm 22:1-21
		Isaiah 53
Jesus was buried	In accordance with Scripture	Isaiah 53
Jesus was resurrected	He was seen by the apostles	Mt 28, Mk 16:9

In Mark 16:16, Jesus said to the disciples; *"He who believes (that I was raised from the dead) and is baptized, will be saved,"* or did he mean; *"He who believes (that I died for the atonement of your sin), will be saved?"* Either or both are possibilities.

There is a big difference between the religions of the pagans and that of the Christians. The earliest religions may have had little or no concept of a permanent life beyond this world. Such concept may have developed as seen from materials being buried with key people in preparation for an afterlife. Christianity, however, is focused on a permanent life, interrupted by the death of the body, and continued existence as a soul, and followed at some point by a resurrected body reunited with the soul. To be reunited with God, Christian theology indicates there must be a belief in the act of God through Jesus, that this resurrection will occur, if we but accept and believe that Jesus' obedience and death brought about that possibility.

About the Authors of the Canon

Who Knew Whom

The Apostles who were eyewitnesses to Jesus' ministry and who wrote, or influenced the writings of the books of the New Testament were Peter, Matthew, John the son of Zebedee, and Jude. Mark was not one of the twelve, but probably witnessed much of Jesus' ministry. Paul was not an eyewitness to Jesus, but he knew Peter and possibly some other eyewitnesses. Luke did not have first-hand experiences with Jesus, but was influenced by Paul and the writings of Mark and Matthew.

Paul (Saul of Tarsus)

Paul was probably the first person to unknowingly write for the Christian Canon. His letters to the churches that he founded probably preceded Mark's gospel by a few years. Paul was not interested in writing history so much as encouraging his churches to be faithful to the new religion.

Paul had spent at least 15 days with Peter in their first meeting (Galatians 1:18). He and Peter met on other occasions including a confrontation in Antioch over Peter's refusal to eat with local Gentiles. Peter had previously eaten with Gentiles and Paul was quite irate with Peter over this. Paul obviously met many of the other Apostles plus James and possibly Jude, the brothers of Jesus. He was an eyewitness to the stoning of Stephen, the first Christian martyr (Acts 7: 54ff).

Paul may have been born in Tarsus perhaps five years or so after Jesus. He was a Hellenistic Pharisee, and according to Acts 22:3 was educated in the temple at Jerusalem by Gamaliel, a wise and respected rabbinical teacher of the law. Paul was an avid defender of the Jewish traditions and actively sought out Jewish heretics that had accepted the new Christian religion.

Saul had been sent to Damascus to extradite more Jewish converts, presumably on authority of the Roman government. On the way he had a vision and a confrontation by Jesus, who said, "Saul, Saul, why do you persecute me (Acts 9:4)?" Saul was stricken blind and had to be led by his companions to the home of a Judas in Damascus. Saul was surely emotionally driven by his conversion experience and his temporary blindness. A disciple named Ananias was sent to Saul after three days to restore his sight.

After his recovery from his blindness, he journeyed into Arabia and preached in various synagogues in the area, often getting himself in trouble because he wasn't trusted as a convert. He visited a number of cities and formed congregations wherever he went, as evidenced by his letters to these churches ca. 51 – 60 C.E.

A traveling companion, Silvanus, probably wrote a number of the Epistles attributed to Paul, but Paul would at least personally write the final paragraph in his own hand. The books clearly ascribed to Paul were[1]: Romans, First and Second Corinthians, Galatians, Philippians, First Thessalonians, and Philemon.

Colossians is probably from Paul based on his mention of Philemon, but the style of the letter is not his. Ephesians is representative of a second generation Christian and the Pastoral Epistles of 1st and 2nd

Timothy and Titus were probably written well after Paul's death. Elaine Pagels[2] of Princeton believes that these books were pseudo-Pauline forgeries in that they opposed the equality of women with men within the church and in society. She says that Paul had a more favorable attitude toward women. Paul, as a Hellenistic, but pharisaic Jew in his early years, typically would have cast women in a role subordinate to men. After his conversion and meetings with the apostles, he may have changed his attitude. Luke, Paul's traveling companion on subsequent trips, certainly espoused equality of women in his writings. Both Luke and Paul would have learned that women were prominent followers and supporters of Jesus. They would have learned that Jesus made no distinction between male and female followers.

Pagels indicates that in the second century, the majority of Christian communities, along with the middle class, generally opposed the equality of women with men in religion[2]. This assuredly was a cultural mindset much more than a religious perspective.

Paul believed that Christ would surely return during his lifetime, so he urged his listeners not to make great changes in their lives. Similarly, Paul was writing to specific audiences and their stage of faith at the time. He was much less interested in history than in helping his newly formed churches grasp a proper meaning of Jesus life and death. At the time of Paul's letters, there were a wide variety of faith positions among the Marcionites, the Ebionites and the Gnostics. Paul's writings were to form the backbone of the proto-orthodox Christians whose views became the basis of the Christian canon in 325 C.E. Paul's letters, as well as the letters of Peter and Jude are full of warnings of heretical teachings by false teachers and prophets. These are probably inferences to beware of the teachings of Gnostics, Marcionites, and Ebionites, among others.

Both Paul and Peter were executed in Rome under the orders of Nero some time soon after the fire that destroyed a portion of Rome. Nero, of course, blamed this tragedy on the Christians. Their executions occurred between 64 and 67 C.E[3].

John Mark

Mark was the first gospel writer, although not one of the twelve disciples, he probably had considerable first-hand knowledge of Jesus. Peter also speaks of Mark as if he knew him face to face. Peter is supposed to have stayed with Mark and his mother at their home after Peter's first release from prison. Peter obviously had a fondness for Mark. According to Peter's writings he infers that Mark was probably quite a bit younger than his fellow disciples.

Mark may have been a teenager at the time of Jesus' arrest, and if he were at Gethsemane, he would have been blown away with fear at that scene. We wonder if he was the young man who ran away naked after Jesus was seized at the garden of Gethsemane (Mark 14:51). If this is true, it is no wonder that he wished to remain anonymous.

Mark was a fellow traveler with Paul and Barnabas on their first missionary trip. He traveled with Barnabas on a missionary trip while Paul traveled with Silas (Acts 15: 36-41).

Mark is thought to have written his Gospel while visiting Peter who was in jail in Rome probably about 67 - 70 C.E. [4], which was about 10 to 15 years after Paul wrote his Epistles, and about 38 years after Jesus' execution. Mark may have been about 60 – 65 years old when he wrote his gospel. He probably did not have document "Q" available to him. Document Q is an inferred written collection of sayings of Jesus, which was written by anonymous authors about the same time, or perhaps a little earlier than Mark's gospel. It is inferred because both Matthew and Luke used the material virtually verbatim in their gospels.

Bishop John Shelby Spong, in his book *Jesus for the Non-Religious* makes a strong argument that Mark's Gospel, and the two that followed, are organized as worship books for the Christian Jews. Mark spaced certain events in his book to be read exactly when the observances of the Jewish Holy days occur. The verses of Mark's gospel cited in Table 6.1 below are specifically aimed at the meaning of the Jewish Holy Days indicated.

Coincidence of Jewish Holy Days with Mark's Gospel Table 6.1			
Holy Day	Month	Subject	Citations in Mark
Rosh Hashanah	Sept	The gathering of the people and John the Baptist and the beginning of Jesus ministry	1:1-15
Yom Kippur	Oct	Atonement & miraculous healings	chaps. 2 & 3
Sukkoth	Oct	Harvest, parable of the sower, Jesus' Galilean ministry	chaps. 5 - 9
Hanukah	Dec	Light of God & the transfiguration	chap. 9
Passover	April	The Exodus & crucifixion	chaps. 14 - 16
Pentecost	June	The giving of the Law	Omitted

Mark covered about 6 ½ months of the Jewish liturgical year with the expectation, according to Spong, that portions of his book would be read every Sabbath with particular topics covered on the Holy days so the events of Jesus' life and His teachings would be seen in the context of Jewish history. Spong concludes that Mark's book was not intended as history so much as it was intended for liturgical use in the Temples.

What Bishop Spong wrote made immediate sense to me. Mark, a Jew, wrote his book primarily for Jews, but in the light and context of Jesus' new message to His people. Mark understood that Jesus was the long expected Messiah sent from God. He anticipated that the Jewish religion would maintain itself and its history and that Jews would incorporate Jesus into their religion.

Mark is also thought to have become a leader of the Christian church in Alexandria, Egypt[5].

   Jude, (half-brother of Jesus)

Jude[6] was said by some to be the twin brother of Jesus since his name was preceded by the title "Didymus" which in Greek means, "twin." Also, he could have been the twin of James, another a half-brother of Jesus [Matt 13:55 & Mk 6:3]. Luke twice refers to Jude as the son of James [Lk 6:16 & Acts 1:13]. Finally, he could have been Thaddeus[7], who seemingly is never mentioned in the gospels [Matt 10:2]. In any event, he is considered to be one of the twelve. Jude wrote a very short letter (before Revelation) between 64 CE and 80 CE warning the new church of the false teachings that had arisen in the 40 years after Jesus crucifixion. Armenian tradition has Jude martyred in Lebanon in 65 CE[7].

It will be easier for you to capture the sequence of the gospels by seeing it diagrammatically in Figure 6.1. This represents my best sequence based on my readings of various sources.

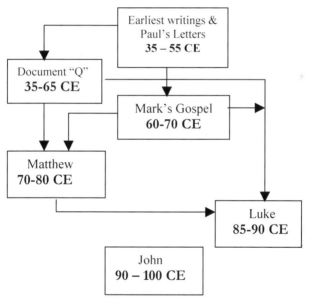

Probable Sequence of the Gospels
Figure 6.1

You will notice that there are no ties to John's Gospel. It contains nothing in common with the other three. It is totally John's creation.

Matthew

The gospel of Matthew was written anonymously. The original manuscript was in Hebrew, probably Aramaic, but the version that was published as our canon today was a Greek copy or translation of the Hebrew. While it cannot be proven that the Apostle Matthew, the former Levi the tax collector, was the author, it is generally considered probable.[8] The fact that the Matthew gospel was written for Jews, and obviously by a Jew, points straight at Matthew.[9,10]

Levi, as Matthew was originally named, worked for the Roman government. He collected taxes for them, but was not paid a salary for his efforts. He was expected to overcharge his clients and glean his own living that way. As a result, he was an outcast, and as a Jew, he was hated all the more as a traitor.   Nonetheless, I suspect that Matthew was a devout, Torah-abiding Jew who practiced his faith obediently.

In spite of his bad reputation, Jesus asked Levi to follow Him, and he did, apparently without hesitation. This is another example of Jesus reaching out to the marginalized and outcasts of society.

Matthew's gospel contains twenty-eight chapters; compared with Mark's sixteen chapters, nearly double the length. Matthew contains about ninety-four percent of   Mark's gospel, with minor emphasis changes directed to Jews.   Then he adds a lot of material that is strictly aimed for Jewish Christians. As an example, Matthew starts with a genealogy of Jesus that shows his lineage through David to Abraham. Matthew wanted to clearly show that Jesus not only was a son of David, but also of Abraham.

There was no birth record of Jesus, so Matthew created one. Who were the reporters in Bethlehem at the birth of Jesus? Well, there were none. The apostles were either not yet born or they were toddlers, just a little older than baby Jesus. Mark didn't write about the birth of Jesus in his gospel. He didn't know anything about it. Matthew however, had to have created a birth story to fulfill some Hebrew Bible prophecies. I expect Matthew may have been five to ten years old when Jesus was born. He should have been well into his adulthood to become a tax collector when he knew Jesus.

Matthew's Christmas Story

If you return to Table 6.2 you see that Matthew refers to four Hebrew scripture passages to create a birth narrative about Jesus. Jesus was probably was born in Nazareth, his parent's home town, and Joseph wouldn't have taken his very pregnant wife on a donkey ride to a city to be counted in a census. She wouldn't have been counted, plus Joseph probably had children at home he wouldn't leave alone.

Jesus Fulfills Hebrew Predictions Table 6.2		
Matthew Ref.	**Subject**	**Hebrew Ref.**
1: 18-25	Birth by a virgin	Isaiah 7:14
2:1-12	Birth in Bethlehem	Micah 5:2
2:13-15	Joseph & Mary flee to Egypt	Hosea 11:1
2:16-18	Herod kills boys age 2 and under	Jeremiah 31:15
4:14-16	Jesus' ministry in Galilee	Isaiah 9:1-2
8:17	Jesus' healings	Isaiah 53:4
12:17-21	Jesus seen as Isaiah's servant	Isaiah 42:1-4
13:35	Jesus speaking in parables	Ps 78:2
21:4-5	Jesus royal entry into Jerusalem	Zech 9:9
27:3-10	Judas regrets the betrayal, returns money	Jeremiah 32:6-8
27:8-10	Judas suicide	Zech 11:12-13

As I would look at the Christmas story and God's entrance into the world in the form of Jesus, there would have been no kings, no shepherds, and no reporters at Jesus' birth. Only the family would have been there plus maybe some relatives. God does not seem to enter human life to the sound of trumpet and fanfare. He does so very quietly and humbly as in a burning bush. No matter, Matthew and Luke wrote to make a point to specific audiences.

Matthew was portraying Jesus as the one who was fulfilling the ancient Laws of God as delivered to Moses and the prophets. None of the material presented in Table 6.2 would have any meaning to Gentiles, but it would to practicing Jews. Matthew wanted his readers to know that Jesus was a Jew and that He was the Messiah that had come to liberate them. By inserting the Sermon on the Mount, Matthew could also portray Jesus as the new and greater Moses who delivered a new set of laws on the mountain.

Don't be dismayed, Jesus was born, but there was nobody around except maybe Joseph's other children. This doesn't make the Bible invalid, it was just Matthew trying to make a point about how this young Jesus fit into the Jewish past. One clue that Luke had seen Matthew's gospel before he wrote his own is that he copied both Matthew's accounts of Jesus' birth and his genealogy and elaborated both accounts. A contradiction in the birth stories is that Matthew has an angel speak to Joseph about Jesus' coming birth as a patriarchal Jew would do, but Luke has Gabriel speak directly to Mary bypassing Joseph entirely.

To give some importance to Jesus' birth, Matthew has some wise priestly types (kings) from the east (Iran) follow a star to Bethlehem to the place where Jesus lay. This wasn't a quick trip because it may have been 1,000 miles or more. That would have taken four to six weeks by camel. The priests were carrying symbolic gifts; gold for a king, frankincense for a priest, and myrrh for someone who was to die. Luke substituted shepherds in place of the priests and he omitted the gifts.

The wise men as we know them, were of the religious caste of Zoroastrianism[11] and could have been of such significance that they nominated, appointed, and/or anointed kings. They were also astrologers and therefore had an interest in the stars.

I believe that Matthew was trying to emphasize that kings came to worship the baby Jesus at birth and that they brought gifts appropriate for a king. Matthew wanted his Jewish readers to understand that Jesus was their new King. Matthew, in retrospect, could see that this king had come to die, as symbolized by the myrrh.

To be politically sensitive to the Gentiles, however, Matthew does indicate that in the Great Commission (Matt 28:18-20) the disciples had a mission to the entire world. Matthew had Document Q available to him, which comprised many of the sayings of Jesus. He and Luke independently incorporated document Q virtually verbatim. This material would be directed to both Jews and Gentiles.

Bishop Shelby Spong indicates that Matthew also follows the liturgical outline of Mark by keeping the same material spaced in such a way to fall on Jewish holy days. However Matthew expands the material to fill a complete liturgical year. Mark had provided no readings for Shavuot (Pentecost) in June, so Matthew inserted the Sermon on the Mount to fall in that period. Shavuot is a celebration of the giving of the Law. Matthew treats the Sermon on the Mount as the new law given by the new Moses. The difference is that Jesus raised the bar on the meaning of the law. No longer was "Thou shalt not commit adultery" the standard, it would be "Do not look upon another with lust in your heart" or you will already have committed adultery. Jesus moved the laws from "acts" to "attitudes." To refrain from the "act" of evil was fine, but to refrain even from the thought of evil, was better.

Matthew's gospel was probably written after the Romans had quelled a Jewish zealot uprising in 68-70 C.E[12]. So it was probably written sometime between 70 – 80 C.E. It was in wide circulation by 90 C.E. Matthew had probably died by about 80 CE, so he may have drafted his gospel after Mark's writings were published ca. 70 CE and it is possible that a follower of Matthew finished or at least published his gospel.

Luke

Luke[13] was born in Antioch, Turkey about the first year of the Common Era. He was an educated man and a physician, said to live in Troas. Luke was not an eyewitness to Jesus' ministry, but did become a traveling companion of Paul and learned much from Paul. He would have been about four to six years younger than Jesus. He would have had Hellenistic cultural influences, and would have spoken and written Greek. He may have been a Hellenistic Gentile who converted to Christianity, possibly under the influence of Paul. If so, he is the only Gentile to have contributed to the New Testament[14]. His gospel certainly indicated a thorough knowledge of the Hebrew Scriptures. Surely he was an educated man and a physician by profession. He obviously traveled with Paul on some of his visits to churches in Asia Minor.

Luke never would have met Jesus nor would have been an eyewitness to events in Jerusalem during Jesus' ministry there. His knowledge is therefore secondhand except for his personal knowledge of the Hebrew Scriptures and worship calendar.

Luke's gospel was the third Gospel written, after Mark's and Matthew's, probably about 80 C.E. Luke is supposed to have died in 84 C.E. at the age of 84[13]. He had copies of both Mark's and Matthew's gospels plus Document Q, which both Matthew and Luke used as source material.

Luke wrote both his own gospel and the book of Acts in tandem and addressed them to some Christian official or patron named Theophilus. While Luke's direct addressee was Theophilus, he was writing to Gentile Christians in general. He seemed to want to put down a logical and coherent history of the life of Jesus and of the progress of the growing church since the resurrection. Much of Acts is focused on Paul. When Luke uses the first person plural "we" it is assumed that he was traveling with Paul, and the text is eyewitness material. Each time the two passed through Troas, the text shifts from first person plural to third person singular suggesting that Luke stayed at home, and he was recording the adventures of Paul alone.

Remember that Mark's gospel was only sixteen chapters long. Luke's gospel contains twenty-four chapters compared with twenty-eight chapters in Matthew's gospel. Luke used seventy-seven percent of Mark's gospel (twelve chapters) while Matthew used about ninety-four percent (fifteen chapters). Both Luke and Matthew devote about six identical chapters of material from Document Q, none of which was in Mark. Luke and Matthew's gospels each contained about six chapters of their own origin.

There is a consensus among scholars that Luke's original gospel was written in Greek, which would have been Luke's native language. Luke takes his first two chapters as a prologue to introducing the ministry of Jesus. He takes Matthew's genealogy that ends with Abraham and expands it another thirty-three generations back to Adam, and thence to the "Son of God," The prologue also includes an expanded discussion of the births of both John the Baptist and Jesus, and the only glimpse of Jesus as a young boy sitting with the rabbis in the Temple at Jerusalem. Luke probably gained this thought from Paul's experience with the rabbis.

From Table 6.2, Bishop Spong sees Luke following a one-year liturgy of the life of Jesus and his teachings to follow the Jewish Holy days. The sequence of his stories would be similar to Matthew's, however the points he wished to emphasize are somewhat different. For example, at Pentecost Jews would celebrate the giving of the Law through Moses. For Luke, the emphasis is God giving to mankind the gift of the Holy Spirit. Bishop Spong makes a logical set of examples for his conclusions.

Why Luke, in particular would be interested in doing this, I don't know, other than the fact that many converts were Jewish and their Holy days would be sacred to them. Luke, like Matthew, was interested in clearly portraying Jesus as the long awaited Jewish Messiah.

Luke also brings women into a much more prominent role as disciples and active followers of Jesus. An example of this is the material on Elizabeth, John the Baptist's mother, which is not found in the other gospels. Also it is interesting to note that in Matthew, the angels speak to Joseph about Mary's impending pregnancy with Jesus, while in Luke, the angel speaks directly to Mary, and Joseph is not a player in that dialogue. The two gospels are totally at odds with each other historically. Each writer may have been expressing himself from a cultural bias. Neither story is factual partly because they are contradictory, but also because it was the social custom to associate a great leader with a virgin birth descended from the gods.

James

James, the author of the five-chapter New Testament book, was probably a Hellenistic convert and a preacher/teacher because his use of the Greek language was so good. It is less likely that he was the son of Zebedee and brother of John, the beloved disciple. Scholars have discounted him as having been the brother of Jesus since that James would not have been facile in Greek.

John, the Son of Zebedee

John the son of Zebedee and brother of James is reputed to be the author of the fourth Gospel, three epistles bearing his name, and the book of Revelation[15]. The Gospel and Revelation show the marks of an editor because the narrative shifts from first person to third person. Since the gospel was written while he was an old man, two things might be deduced; first, that his works were written over time and edited later, second, that someone helped him write the books, assuming he was 80 or more when they were made public.

John was the last apostle to die, so I expect he was perhaps 10-14 years younger than Jesus when called to be His disciple (possibly at age 19). He and Mark might have been about the same age. John died about 68 years after Jesus so that would place his death about the year 97 C.E. or so, when he might have been about 90 years old. It is said that John had to be carried to the temple to worship in his final years. That might further indicate that he was a nonagenarian.

John and his brother James were half-cousins of Jesus since their mother, Salome, was Mary's sister[16]. He was obviously an eyewitness to Jesus' ministry and after the crucifixion; he ministered with Peter, who referred to him as a pillar of the church (Gal 2:9). John was referred to as the disciple whom Jesus loved. This would indicate that John, being younger than Jesus, looked up to Him with great admiration and affection.

The gospel of John bears little resemblance to the synoptic gospels that preceded it. He emphasizes and starts his gospel with the fact that Jesus is God and of the same substance as God. He was begotten in earthly form, but was with the Father God in Spirit from the beginning. John portrays love as being the essence of God and the chief objectives of believers. John only, describes what Jesus revealed in private, or with the other disciples, when He talked about Himself.

John was of course, a Jew, and he saw Jesus as the long awaited Jewish Messiah, but John's most famous passage is 3:16 in which he states that eternal life comes through belief in Jesus the Christ as the ultimate act of love on God's part for mankind.

Most scholars place John's Gospel at 90 – 100 CE. Since he authored the Gospel, three letters and Revelation, it might be deduced that these were written over a period of time, not necessarily in the order presented in the New Testament. Also, since there is some evidence of editing Revelation, it is safe to assume that book was published after John's death. I could believe that the letters were written first because he indicates he is healthy enough to want to come and visit the receiver in person. I could believe that the gospel followed the letters and that Revelation was written last.

Many scholars believe that the four gospels were developed in three stages. The first stage was comprised of the original experience of the writer, followed by amendments and additions of material taken from other sources, such as Document Q. The final stage would have been the editing and translation of the amended gospel performed much later by friends or followers of the original writer, and/or by church fathers. The final version is what we have today.

Non-orthodox belief systems were prevalent at the time of John such as held by the Marcionites, Gnostics and Ebionites, and John warned against falling victim to false ideologies. These ideologies were probably well formed after 40 CE and certainly before Matthew's gospel was circulated in 85-90 CE.

John was not at all interested in writing about the historical Jesus, but rather whom Jesus was, following from Peter's confession. The Jews got the message that God had visited them in the form of Jesus, and everything else was of little consequence. Mark did not have this mature perspective, nor did Matthew or Luke pick up on it, as did John.

John lived in Ephesus and was pastor of the church there, but he also helped establish churches in other nearby regions. He is the only apostle alleged to have died of old age, all the others having been martyred by the Roman government.

Document "Q"

You will not find Document Q in your local library. It doesn't exist, but it may have. Conservative and Fundamentalist Christians are apt to say it never existed. Modern scholars suggest that such a document once existed by inference of a study of Matthew and Luke. They contain material, primarily sayings of Jesus that they included in their gospels, in the same order, and for the most part, with close or exact wording. Matthew wrote in advance of Luke. They did not consult with each other on their writings, however Luke must have seen Matthew's work while writing his own since he expanded on material Matthew wrote. Because they included identical material in their books strongly implies that there was available to both of them, a common document, which had to be in written form. This is called Document Q.

The non-canonical Gospel of Didymus Judas Thomas contains one hundred fourteen sayings of Jesus some of which are repeated in a different form in Document Q, Matthew, Luke, and John[17,18]. The Thomas Gospel is obviously of Gnostic origin and theology, but someone decided it was important to capture the wisdom of Jesus. The words "Didymus" and "Thomas" both mean "twin." The scroll found at Nag Hamadi was written in Coptic, but earlier versions were written in Greek. The grammar however, is typical of Aramaic writing since no conjunctions are used[19]. I assume that Document Q was written before the Gospel of Thomas and that Gnostics wrote both documents.

Catholic tradition suggests that Jude, the brother of Jesus, may have been the author of Thomas. He certainly would have been familiar with the sayings of Jesus. However, it is doubtful that Jude would have been a Gnostic even if they believed that Jesus was the source of secret knowledge that the Gnostics looked for. What makes sense to me is that Jude could have written down some of the sayings of his brother Jesus in Aramaic, and that early Gnostics may have copied them into Q and Thomas in Greek.

Elaine Pagels places the authorship of "Q" about 60 C.E. before Mark wrote his gospel. Bart Ehrman, on the other hand places the writing in the second century after all the synoptic gospels had been written.

Other proponents of the Q document have suggested it was written at the earliest by 50 C.E. It would make sense that the oral statements made by Jesus were gradually compiled and written down by this time since the various forms of the new church were being codified at least by twenty years after Jesus' death. In later years Q was probably amended by adding some narrative material including the story of John the Baptist, Jesus' temptations, and two miracle stories of Jesus.[20] Either way the work is symptomatic of various writings being published in the decades following Christ's death and the wide variety of opinions about what Christ's appearance on earth meant.

There had to have been a large body of oral traditions that was spread about in the early church. I suspect as time passed after Jesus' death and resurrection, followers advancing in years, would capture these traditions in writing. They would surely be developing some liturgies for their worship. The early writings probably consisted of sayings of Jesus, histories and significant events that were remembered, advice to new converts, and assuredly some liturgies to be followed in new worship settings[21]. Not all of these writings would have made it to press, so to speak. Many probably were never copied. Other later documents may have been compilations of early works and Document Q might have been copied as an accepted good work. It obviously would have had wide circulation to be available to both Matthew and Luke.

Other Christian Belief Systems

As the Jewish-Christian and Gentile-Christian churches were emerging, there arose a fairly wide variety of belief systems, which contradicted each other. These systems carried into the fourth century before Constantine ordered the Bishops to convene and settle on a single canon. All writings of heretical belief systems were to be destroyed and not kept upon penalty of death, according to Constantine.

Much of the information presented on the various groups cited below come from the lectures of Dr. Bart D. Ehrman of the University of North Carolina. The primary groups holding to differing beliefs were:

- The Ebionites
- The Marcionites
- The Gnostics
- The Proto-Orthodox

The Ebionites[22,23]

The Ebionites were a Jewish-Christian sect that existed in the first millennium and were fairly widespread, although concentrated in Palestine and Galilee. Their basic tenet was that to be a Christian, one must also adhere to the Jewish rites and laws. Their basic beliefs were:

1. There was one God only
2. Jesus was a prophet like Moses, but not divine
3. Observance of Jewish rites and Laws was mandatory
4. They followed the Gospel of Matthew only as their authority
5. They looked upon Paul as a heretic.

These were ascetic Jews forsaking wealth and taking poverty upon themselves as an act of strict obedience to liturgical laws.

The Marcionites[24]

Marcion was a Christian lay theologian who lived ca. 110-160 C.E. in Sinope, Turkey. His father was a leader of the Christian church in Turkey, while Marcion himself, was a wealthy ship owner. About 138 C.E. Marcion went to Rome and became a church member there. Because he was wealthy, he was able to give large sums of money to the church, which propelled him into prominence in the Roman church. He was articulate and learned and studied the Christian teachings. He was very much influenced by the writings of Paul and essentially felt that Jesus had superseded all of the Hebrew laws and teachings. He gathered a large following, but ultimately was considered a heretic by the church at Rome and was excommunicated.

Marcionite beliefs can be summarized as follows:

1. There were two Gods:
   - The God of Creation was bad, being cruel and merciless
   - The God of Jesus was good, merciful, loving and kind

2. Jesus was divine
3. The Jewish rites, laws and observances were made null and void by Jesus' teachings
4. Paul was the true Apostle
5. Marcion's canon was his version of the gospel of Luke plus ten of Paul's epistles
6. Other teachings of Marcion were:
   - Christians should not eat meat, fish, eggs, etc. or drink wine
   - They should avoid contact with the opposite sex
   - They should not bear arms as soldiers or guards
   - Marriage was to be scorned and the birth of children was forbidden (They believed the end of time was soon to come, as Paul believed)

Gnosticism[25, 26]

Gnosticism seems to come in a variety of differing beliefs, but its mainstream tenets were:
1. There is a hierarchy of Gods, led by a supreme God, with lower tier gods, one of whom was the flawed creator god
2. The flawed creator god created the earth and the souls created therein became imprisoned in earthly bodies that were morally flawed
3. Jesus was an emanation from the Supreme God to bring "gnosis," (secret knowledge) that would allow people to escape from their evil bodies.

Elaine Pagels believes that Paul leaned toward Gnosticism since he agreed with the denigration of the flesh in favor of cultivation of the spirit. I suspect he would have disagreed with the concept of multiple gods, having been a pharisaic, monotheistic Jew.

Early Christian Commentators

So as to portray a picture of early confusion and uncertainty of the correct belief system to be followed by new Christians, I'd like to write about three early students of scripture and authors of differing viewpoints some two and three centuries after the death of Jesus. The earliest was Origen of Alexandria, Egypt who lived 185 – 254 C.E. The second will be Arius, also from Alexandria who lived ca. 256 - 336 C.E. and was just about nine or ten years older than Eusebius, my final subject. Arius was to be declared a heretic by the organized church based on his views of the Trinity.

Origen[27,28,29]

Origen was born during the reign of Roman Emperor Septimus Severus (185/6 C.E.) and died during the reign of Gallus (254/5 C.E.). This was a period when the Roman Empire was under attack from barbarians from the north plus its own internal moral and economic decay. The government blamed their problems on the Christians and persecuted them and/or those whom they thought would be a threat to the empire.

Origen was born to devout Christian parents and was intensely educated both in Greek philosophy and Christian doctrine. At age seventeen, Origen became headmaster and sole teacher of the Christian Catechetical School in Alexandria. It should be noted that Gnosticism flourished during his lifetime. One of Origen's early challenges was to prepare a refutation of Gnosticism in his publication *On First Principles.* The Treatise was prepared in four books with subjects as follows:

Book 1 – The Trinity, reason, and the angels
Book 2 - The world, man (including the incarnation of
         Logos, the Christ), the soul, free will, and
         eschatology.
Book 3 - Sin and Redemption
Book 4 - The Scriptures

The key themes in this Treatise are:
- Free will
- The educational value of history
- The restoration of all beings

Origen began *On First Principles* with a discussion of his concept of the Trinity. He calls his divine hierarchical triad by the names

"Father," "Christ," and "Holy Spirit." He further went on to explain that the God-Father is superior to every being that exists, for He imparts to each one from his own existence that which each one is. The Son is second to the Father and superior to rational creatures alone. The Holy Spirit is still less and dwells within the saints alone. Origen reasoned in Platonic fashion that God is a perfect unity, complete unto Himself, without body – a purely spiritual mind, personal and active. It followed for Origen, that there existed with God from the beginning, a second entity, Christ the Son, the Logos or Wisdom of God. Emanating from the Son, was the Holy Spirit, the third and lowest form of God related to Christ as if He were a son.

At this time there was no defined orthodox canon, but Origen's thoughts were among many differing opinions on the nature of God and His relationship to mankind.

Origen went on to theorize about souls and their fall. He thought that God's first creation was a limited group of rational souls meant to be in close proximity to Him, with the intention that they explore the divine mysteries in endless contemplation. We would call this creation, "the Angels." He posits that they grew weary of this contemplation, since they had their own free wills, and some fell away from God. The fall was not a result of their imperfection, but of a misuse of free will. The only soul that did not fall away was Christ. He remained faithful and close to the Father by His supreme act of free choice.

As the fallen separated from God they changed from pure spiritual beings into tangible bodies. When the fallen achieve salvation they return to a state of pure "mind" and spiritual body.

Origen's concept of salvation was that all souls were to be reunited with God. There would not be, "some in" and some others "suffering in hell." He believed that God's love is so powerful, that the human intellect will never freely choose oblivion over living in proximity to God. He wrote that the process of salvation might require considerably more time than the length of a physical lifetime. He thought that there would be further education and nurturing after death until all souls, including the devil himself, would freely choose to live in obedience with God.

Origen was creative in his theology. He was influenced by the philosophies of Socrates and Plato. He was not a Gnostic, and did not believe the body was an evil creation entrapping an immortal soul. He saw the body as a beautiful representation of one's unique soul, which is an image of God Himself. His philosophies were accepted by a majority of the church into the sixth century.

In 545 C.E. some of his teachings were declared anathema and heretical by the council in Constantinople. Those teachings included:
- His hierarchical view of the Trinity
- The preexistence of souls
- The concept of a universal salvation

Based on the findings of anathema against many of his writings, the church ordered that they be destroyed.

Arius[30,31,32]

Arius was born just a year or two after Origen died. Probably he was a Libyan. Arius lived ca. 256 – 336 C.E. and studied in Antioch under St. Lucian. Arius was a man of pure morals, ascetic behavior, and great intellect, and became a Bishop of Alexandria sometime after 313 C.E.

Arius developed a view that there was one God, indivisible, and that Jesus was of "like substance," (*homoi ousion)* but not the same substance (*homo ousion)* as God. He believed that Jesus was begotten of the Father. Arius and his followers believed that if Jesus were of the same substance as the Father, that there would be two Gods. The Arians held to the Jewish tradition of a single true God.

Constantine excommunicated Arius after the Council in 325 C.E., for beliefs the Bishops held as heretical. His works were ordered burned. Constantine readmitted him to the church about three years later, but Arius died soon thereafter from poison, supposedly fed him by his opposers.

Eusebius of Caesarea[33]

Eusebius of Caesarea is another name that pops up prominently in the development of the Christian canon. He is not to be confused with Eusebius, Bishop of Nicomedia who lived during the same period and was a proponent of Arius' views. He was reputed to be the father of church history during his lifetime of ca. 265-339 C.E. Eusebius was primarily a historian, rather than a theologian or leader, but he did rise to become Bishop of Caesarea Maritima some time after 313. Eusebius had the attention of Emperor Constantine and he was an active participant in the Council at Nicaea in 325.

Eusebius was an avid student of the scriptures. He and Pamphilus prepared a textual criticism of the Septuagint (Greek version of the Hebrew Testament) as well as the books of the New Testament. He provided, perhaps the first version, of a set of comparative tables of the four gospels. These Eusebian canons survived into the Middle Ages. One of his great works was his *Church History*. This was the first history of the Christian church, chronologically organized from the time of the Apostles to his present day. It was correlated with the reigns of the Roman Emperors, the bishops and teachers of the church; and included the relationships of Jews, Christians, and heretical groups.

Eusebius was heavily influenced by the writings of Origen and Arius. He believed in one absolute and sovereign God, and that Jesus proceeded from God, but was subordinate to Him (like substance). Eusebius followed Origen's philosophy that the Holy Spirit proceeded from Jesus. After being threatened with excommunication by Bishop Alexander of Alexandria, Eusebius did the politically expedient thing and agreed to the Nicene Creed (which he provided the original draft).

The Early Creeds[34]

The church leaders did produce creeds in the third and fourth centuries to help unify a belief system. The Apostles Creed and the Nicene Creed are the two chief creeds and they are somewhat close in nature. The authorship of the Apostles Creed is unknown, but it probably was born in Rome. Eusebius wrote a draft of the Nicene

Creed and after considerable modifications, it became the prime output of the Council of Nicaea in 325. Some scholars dispute this because the two were so markedly different.

The Apostles Creed

The traditional Apostles Creed reads as follows:

I believe in God the Father Almighty, Maker of heaven and earth, and in Jesus Christ his only son our Lord, who was conceived by the Holy Ghost, born of the Virgin Mary, suffered under Pontius Pilate, was crucified, dead, and buried; he descended into hell; the third day he rose again from the dead; he ascended into heaven, and sits on the right hand of God Almighty, from thence he shall come to judge the quick and the dead.

I believe in the Holy Ghost, the holy catholic church; the communion of saints; the forgiveness of sins; the resurrection of the body; and the life everlasting. Amen

This creed was written about the end of the second century and is consistent with orthodox beliefs from about 100 C.E. and later.

The reader can now compare this with the draft creed of Eusebius written for, and submitted to the Council at Nicaea in 325.

The Creed of Caesarea (by Eusebius)

We believe in One God, the Father of All Governing, Creator of everything visible and invisible; and in one Lord Jesus Christ, the Word [Logos] of God, God from God, Light from Light, Life from Life, the only begotten Son, the first born of all creation, begotten of the Father before all time, by whom also everything came into being, who for our salvation became incarnate and lived among men. He suffered, and rose the third day, and ascended to the Father, and will come again in Glory to judge the living and the dead.

We believe also in one Holy Spirit.

Eusebius seems to indicate that Jesus was the very first creation of God, before the beginning of time, and that subsequent creation came through Jesus. His purpose was to redeem us from sin and to judge people at the end of time. There are hints of Origen's philosophy, but they are not clearly elucidated as Origen explained them.

The Council of Nicea

Constantine I, Emperor of Rome was converted from Paganism to Christianity, but was generally uninformed about its beliefs. He was not baptized until he was on his deathbed. He was very much aware of the dispute betweens Arians and Orthodox Bishops on the divinity of Christ. He did accede to make Christianity the state religion of the Roman Empire however, one pre-requisite was that the church Bishops unify the various beliefs of Christian sects and in particular, Arianism, and produce a single canon that all Christians would follow. As a result, 318 Bishops together with their entourages, not to exceed five, met from May to July, 325 to deal with the issues. To liken this council to a present day smoke-filled political caucus meeting would not be a stretch to me. I sense that positions were taken very firmly, and that arguments and shouting abounded.

The primary output of the Council were:

- The Nicene Creed
- Twenty Canons dealing with issues of the day
- The method to determine when Easter was to be celebrated

The Nicene Creed as Agreed by the Council

It should be understood that the creed developed at Nicaea was specifically worded to refute the premise of Arius that Jesus was begotten by God and had a beginning, and that he was of similar substance to God (homoi ousion), but not of the same essence of God (homo ousion). The creed was written as follows:

We believe in one God, the Father all governing, creator of all things visible and invisible; and in one Lord Jesus Christ, the Son of God, begotten of the Father as only begotten, that is, from the essence of the Father, God from God, Light from Light, true God from true God, begotten not created, of the same essence as the Father, through whom all things came into being, both in Heaven and in earth; Who for us men and for our salvation came down and was incarnate, becoming human.   He suffered and the third day he rose, and ascended into the heavens, and he will come to judge both the living and the dead.

We believe in the Holy Spirit.

But, those who say, once he was not, or he was not before his generation, or he came to be out of nothing, or who assert the he, the Son of God, is of a different hypostasis or ousia, or that he is a creature, or changeable, or mutable, the Catholic and Apostolic Church anathematizes them.

This is not the version we find in our church hymnals or prayer books today, but you can clearly see the anti-Arianism statement. Arianism still lingered for another half century until it finally was let go.

In 381 the Creed was modified at Constantinople by the council of 150 Fathers to drop the section on anathema and to add the concepts of the *Virgin Mary, of Pontius Pilate, of a single baptism for the remission of sins, and affirmed the deity of the Holy Spirit.* This version is much closer to that which most churches use today.

The Constantinopolitan Creed (Creed of 150 Fathers)

We believe in one God, the Father all governing, creator of heaven and earth, of all things visible and invisible; and in one Lord Jesus Christ, the only begotten Son of God, begotten from the Father before all time, light from Light, true God from true God. Begotten not created, of the same essence as the Father through Whom all things came into being, Who for us men and because of our salvation came down from heaven, and was incarnate by the Holy Spirit and the Virgin Mary and became human.   He was crucified for us under Pontius Pilate, and suffered and was buried, and rose the third day, according to the Scriptures, and ascended to heaven, and sits on the right hand of the Father, and will come again with glory to judge the living and the dead. His Kingdom shall have no end.

And we believe in the Holy Spirit, the Lord and life-giver, who proceeds from the Father, who is worshipped and glorified together with the Father and Son, who spoke through the prophets; and in one, holy, catholic, and apostolic church. We confess one baptism for the remission of sins. We look forward to the resurrection of the dead and the life of the world to come. Amen.

Over the centuries the church and its various denominations have written other creeds, confessions, catechisms and made statements to further define its belief systems. For almost all Christian churches, however the Nicene Creed, as modified in 381 is as close to a consensual creed as there is. Its basic principles are:

- Jesus Christ is of the same essence as the Father and coexisted without a beginning.

- The Holy Spirit is God in a different form, but of the same essence, without a beginning, and forms the third person of the Trinity.

- Jesus was born of a virgin and the Holy Spirit and became human.
- That sins must be atoned for, and that Jesus made the sacrifice for that atonement by dying as a perfect human being.

- Jesus was raised bodily from the dead
- Jesus future role is that of judge
- That there is a single universal church, which proceeded from the Apostles that we bear allegiance to as Christ's family of saints.

Within the creed we can see the Matthewan expression "*according to the scriptures,*" the Jewish notion that the Messiah's appearance had been predicted for centuries by the earlier prophets.

The church fathers over the centuries questioned in their own minds what the scriptures said, what the meaning of Jesus' presence in our lives meant, and what the message of the Apostles was. This process took about 400 years, and essentially has continued ever since, but the main document that represents current day Christian belief is the Nicene Creed.

I have recited this creed hundreds of times without question, but in my later years have come to consider, "wait a minute, I don't believe all of that." So instead of just leaving myself with what I don't believe, I must delve into what I do believe and what makes sense to me as I experience God. I encourage you to do the same.

We will move next from the unified church in 325 C.E. to the reformed and divided church of the current day. We will see that power and myopia helped corrupt the church during the Middle Ages. Our objective is to see how we can reunify the Christian Church.

FOOTNOTES

[1] Wikipedia, *Paul of Tarsus, p 10, 15,16*
[2] Pagels, Elaine, *The Gnostic Gospels,* Vintage Publishers, 1989, p.62
[3] Wikipedia, *Paul of Tarsus, p 9*
[4] Lactanius, John Crysostom, *Of the Manner in which Persecutors Died*
[5] Wikipedia, *Mark the Evangelist, pp 1&2*
[6] Jerome H. Neyrey, *2 Peter, Jude,* Anchor Bible Reference Library, Doubleday, 1993, p.44
[7] Catholic Online, *St. Jude Thaddeus,* p1
[8] Wikipedia, *Matthew the Evangelist*
[9] www.abu.nb.ca/NTIntro, *The Gospel of Matthew*
[10] Catholic Encyclopedia, *St. Matthew*
[11] Boyce, Mary, *A History of Zoroastrianism: The Early Period,* (Brill, 1989, 2nd Ed.,) Vol. 1, pp. 10-11, online
     Boyce, Mary, *Zoroastrians; their religious beliefs and practices,* (Routledge, 2001, 2nd Ed.), p 48, online
[12] www.abu.nb.ca/NTIntro, *The Gospel of Matthew,* pp 4&5
[13] Wikipedia, *Luke the Evangelist p 1,2*
[14] *Encyclopedia Britannica,* Micropedia, vol7. p. 554-555, 1998
[15] Wikipedia, *Gospel of John,* pp 1-4
[16] www.allaboutjesuschrist.org, *John the Apostle,* p1
[17] Ehrman, Dr. Bart D., *DVD Lectures From Jesus to Constantine,*

FOOTNOTES (CON'D)

18. Ehrman, Dr. Bart D., *Lost Christianities*, Oxford University Press, 2003

19. Wikipedia, *Gospel of Thomas*, pp 1 &7

20. Atlantic Monthly Online, *The Search for a Non-Frills Jesus, Charlotte Allen, Dec. 1996*

21. Spong, Bishop John Shelby, *Jesus for the Non-Religious*, ch. 18

22. Wikipedia, *Ebionites*, p1-4

23. Ehrman, Dr. Bart D., *Lost Christianities*, Oxford University Press, 2003

24. Wikipedia, *Marcion of Sinope*, p.1-2

25. Wikipedia, *Gnosticism*

26. Ehrman, Dr. Bart D., *Lost Christianities*, Oxford University Press, 2003

27. Wikipedia, *Origen*, p. 1-11

28. www.iep.utm.edu, Internet Encyclopedia of Philosophy, *Origen of Alexandria*

29. Catholic Encyclopedia, *Origen and Origenism*

30. Wikipedia, *Arius*, p. 1-7

31. Arian-Catholic.org, *Arius of Alexandria, Priest and Martyr*

32. Wikipedia, *Arianism*, p.1-6

33. Wikipedia, *Eusebius of Alexandria*, p.1-5

34. Leith, John H., *Creeds of the Churches, Doubleday & Company, Inc.* 1963

CHAPTER 7

THE DEVELOPMENT OF THE CHRISTIAN CHURCH

If you want to understand your faith,
you must question it and not accept it as presented.
Search out your own answers and then you will understand.

Introduction

Power and corruption crept into the unified church as it became incestuously tied to the state (Rome). The church started a series of crusades, in part to convert people, and in part to combat Islam, which had taken hold of Jerusalem and the Middle East. Intolerance grew up such that inquisitions were held to ferret out heretics that did not conform to church beliefs. Finally, the Reformation arose and the church was again divided.

In this chapter I show the doctrines around which the church was formed and the dogma that drove it apart. In order to reunify the Christian Church, we must clearly understand what originally bound it together, and what has separated it. My feeling is that Christians will never reconcile their differing opinions, but can unify around Christianity's core beliefs, leaving aside other dogma. Arguments as to whether the Pope is infallible when speaking "ex-cathedra," or about transubstantiation and other matters are absolutely academic if society collapses around us. The church needs to focus outward, not inward. The key reason for unification is to build a voice strong enough to combat the evil that has invaded our worldwide societies.

Persecution of Christians

Nero accused Christians falsely for starting the great fire in Rome in 64 C.E. For 250 years thereafter Christians were harassed or persecuted for their refusal to worship the Roman Emperor. Emperor Diocletian oversaw the Great Persecution of Christians during the years 303-311 wherein many were arrested, tortured or thrown into the arena for sport. It was Emperor Galerius who ended this and granted the privilege of Christians to practice their religion.

The Christian Church is Formalized

Disparate religions

While Christianity grew in the first four centuries of the Common Era, offshoot religions also existed, each with a differing position on whom God was and whom Jesus was. In the first century Gnostics, Ebionites, Arians, and Marcionites developed, each with a different set of beliefs. In the third century Manichaeism[1] developed from one of the Persian Gnostic religions. Zoroastrianism[2] also emerged from the philosophy and teachings of the prophet Zoroaster. This also is a Mideastern religion, which spread from Iran to India and China. Their supreme being is Ahura Mazda therefore the religion is also referred to as Mazdaism.   They have some similar beliefs to Christianity in that they expect their god to defeat chaos (evil) and that the dead will be raised to a happy life with Mazda.

Constantine I

Young Constantine[3] was born in 272 C.E. in what is now Serbia, where his mother Helena exposed him to Christianity during his formative years.   When he was 40 in 312 C.E. he allegedly experienced a heavenly vision before leading troops into a battle at Milvian Bridge. The sign in the heavens showed a cross with the words *"in hoc signo, vinces"* (by this sign, conquer). Constantine had his men mark their shields with the Christian symbol "Chi-Rho." They were victorious and Constantine went on to claim the Emperorship as his own.

A year later Constantine issued the Edict of Milan announcing the official toleration of Christianity. He did not make it a state religion, but forbade the persecution of Christians and he returned property to Christians, which had been confiscated during the years of persecution. The state became religion-neutral although Constantine himself declared himself a Christian at this point. The empire was still primarily pagan in 312.

The Council at Nicea – 325 C.E.[4,5,6]

After Constantine decided to become a Christian he became the patron of the religion. He had churches built and promoted Christians to positions of rank within the state. He had pagans pay for the new property and structures of the Christians. Other reforms that he ordered were the end of crucifixions, and better treatment of prisoners. In 321 he declared that Sunday would be an official day of rest.

Arianism was fairly widespread in Europe and was a competing, but contradictory sect of Christianity. Arians believed that Jesus did not exist before He was begotten of the Father in human form. While Jesus was considered to be of like substance as the Father, he was held to be a subordinate being. This was the position that Eusebius and Arius and their followers held. The proto-orthodox held to a Trinitarian view.

Constantine ordered that an ecumenical council be held in May 325 to formalize an official Christian position. Over 300 Bishops from the eastern empire and a few from the west came to Nicea, Turkey (now Isnik, Turkey). At the council Eusebius argued the Arian position, but was shouted down. The council developed the Nicene Creed, that clearly placed Jesus as coexistent with the Father for all times and of equal substance with Him. Anti-Arian statements were placed in the creed to make the proto-orthodox position very clear. The unity of the Father and the Son was made clear at the beginning of the creed and words were inserted after "the Son is begotten" namely, "from the Father and not made." The council had affirmed the belief system of the majority of Christian churches and had officially codified the orthodox position in the Nicene Creed. Arianism was immediately declared heretical, and those not confessing the Creed were excommunicated and stripped of priestly positions.

Constantine's efforts launched the official Christian church. While he let Christianity and paganism coexist for some years, toward the end of his reign he sought to destroy paganism. Emperor Theodosius made Christianity the official state religion. The church and state were melded together. This was probably a reasonable and necessary act to take, but it was also the beginning of trouble.

With that legitimacy, the church grew in power and wealth virtually equal to the state. Church power was centralized in Rome and a bureaucracy was established. When the Western Roman Empire collapsed, the church saw an opportunity to fill the power vacuum that was created. The church took the position that the Pope was the direct emissary of God. He had the power of excommunication and the power to declare people to be doomed to hell after death or to be taken to Heaven. To the peasant this power was frightening. The populace believed in Heaven and Hell, and they didn't want to be consigned to Hell, therefore they obeyed the church, which soon ruled by mortal fear.

From the fourth through the eleventh centuries church power continued to grow, solidify, and spread. During this period nation states were tribal and not strong, the people were illiterate, and there was no central government. As nations ultimately developed centralized rule and power, the feudal system came into place. Land was given to wealthy land barons by the reigning monarchs in exchange for the protection of feudal armies provided by the barons.

Since only the clergy and a few aristocrats were educated, the clergy were employed by the state to keep records and write proclamations etc. They became incestuously tied to the state.

The church acquired property and local bishops gained power and wealth. At the height of its power, the papacy held that it had not only spiritual power, but also power over all temporal matters including matters of science, as well as matters of state. The papacy felt it had the right to crown or depose kings, and it had the right of excommunication to condemn anyone to hell, including kings.

.

The church acquired its wealth by taxing the people ten percent of their income (the tithe). Peasants who worked on church land did so without pay. They were charged if the church performed the rites of baptism, marriage, or burial. With this money the church built schools to educate its clergy and massive cathedrals and churches. These construction projects employed thousands of guild workers, so in many ways, the church was at the center of the lives of the tradesmen.

However, at the height of its power corruption crept in. Positions of clerical authority were bought and sold. Incompetent priests were given roles in the church. Clergy lived in luxury and overlooked their priestly vows, and the church began to sell indulgences to forgive sins and other indiscretions as a means of raising money.

During the latter stages of this same period, art and science began to flourish and literacy grew among the people. As nations grew in strength they resisted the authority of the papacy. Patriotism grew and even local clergy began to grumble about authority from Rome. Kings like Philip IV of France and later, Henry VIII of England, refused to have Popes interfere in state affairs. Kings felt that they were not only heads of state, but also heads of their national church. Roman church councils also felt that the office of the pope had too much power and authority and sought that role for themselves. Inevitably, Roman papal authority diminished in distant countries and it reluctantly focused its attention primarily on Italy.

The Investiture Controversy[7]

During the 11th and 12th centuries a political battle arose between the church and various nations over the rights to appoint bishops and abbots. After the collapse of the Roman Empire and before the 11th century, the Church theoretically appointed bishops and abbots to open positions. In fact, however, since the clergy were educated and literate, many were employed by the state in positions of some authority. So candidates for church office were actually working for kings or their deputies. Kings started the practice of selling positions of authority in the church so they could gather handsome sums of money and large tracts of land in exchange for the appointment. The practice was called simony and it took place in England as well as in Europe.

It had been the custom in the Roman Empire that the Emperor would appoint the pope and the pope would crown various emperors. In 1059, when six-year-old Henry IV became King of Germany (which also included Italy at the time), the Gregorian reformers took advantage of his youth to form the College of Cardinals who would appoint future popes.

In 1075 Pope Gregory VII decreed that the church alone had the sole authority to appoint church officials, taking this authority away from the state. He also stopped the practice of simony. A battle of thrust and parry was started between Rome and the now matured Henry IV who appointed his chaplain as the Bishop of Milan while at the same time the church had their own appointee for the post. The pope countered by excommunicating the king and deposing him. The German aristocracy supported the pope for their own selfish reasons, and ultimately appointed Rudolph von Rheinfeld as king. In 1081 Henry captured and killed the rival Rudolph and went on to invade Rome, hoping to install a friendlier pope, Clement III. Friendly Normans of southern Italy rescued pope Gregory, but sacked Rome in the process.

Succeeding popes eroded the power of the kings over the next several decades, and the controversy was settled in 1107.

The Crusades[8,9]

While this turf battle was going on between the papacy and the European monarchs, trouble was brewing in the Middle East. After 610 C.E., the prophet Muhammad[10,11] had established the Islamic religion and had helped the conversion of Arab tribes from their polytheistic beliefs to the worship of the one God, Allah. The new Islamic religion developed armies to protect themselves against the infidels. Muslims grew in power and influence and fought infidels and Christians alike and ultimately took over the Holy Lands including Jerusalem. When the Muslim Seljuk Turks started encroaching on the Eastern Orthodox Byzantine territory early in the eleventh century, Byzantine Emperor Alexius I requested armed help from Pope Urban II. Understand that the Eastern Orthodox and the Roman churches were both Christian, but with slightly differing viewpoints. That Alexius asked for help from Rome was a move of desperation on his part. The Pope was all too pleased to defend the Christian realm. The Muslims had destroyed the Church of the Holy Sepulcher and had persecuted and killed many Christian pilgrims who traveled to Jerusalem. This was the incentive to help the rival Byzantine Christians.

Toward the end of the first millennium and into the eleventh century there had been a lot of internal fighting in Europe over religious differences and political fighting among nation-states. There was an excess of religious fervor at the time. Kings and lords had experienced armies ready and eager to fight for the Christian religion.

Pope Urban II thought hard about the prospects of spilling blood over the faith, but he took advantage of the current fervor and authorized the first crusade as a "Just War" in 1096. This war was to stop the advance of Islam and restore Jerusalem into Christian control. As such, the pope directed that soldiers take a vow of allegiance to the cause and they would receive a cross from the church to be sown onto their tunics. They would be called "soldiers of the cross." The pope provided incentive to the soldiers by indicating that any killed in battle would be absolved of all sins and immediately be taken into heaven. This was no small incentive to these fighters, many of whom assuredly led very sinful lives.

Pope Urban II started a period of close to 200 years during which nine major crusades; primarily to retake the holy land, but also to convert non-Christians, were conducted by various armies authorized by the Popes at the time.

Thousands died, including many innocent Christians during the nine crusades to the Holy Lands. The Eastern Orthodox ceased to trust the Roman Church for some time. The positive result was that trade was established between the eastern and western empires and that eastern art, science, and medicines were brought to the west.

There were other crusades as well as those to the Holy Lands. Crusades were conducted in Spain and Portugal as well as Europe. The Cathars, a self-proclaimed Christian group who generally followed the gospel of John emerged from the Byzantine Empire and flourished in Southeastern France and Northern Italy as well as the Balkans. The Cathars[12], primarily referred to as Abilgenses, were middle class trades people who led ascetic lives. They did not lie, take lives, nor swear oaths. They believed in a good spiritual God and also in His adversary, the creator god. They followed Gnostic beliefs in that they felt that all matter was evil and also that power and love were totally incompatible. They did not believe in a church hierarchy, nor did they build church buildings. They chose poverty and plain worship. They disagreed with the tenets of the Roman Catholic Church, particularly about procreative sex, and they disagreed that the church should have the power and wealth that it had. They saw men and women as equals, as did Luke. They followed the scriptures closely and they were vegetarians. In their time they were popular, particularly among literate and liberal theologians. Many Catholics defected from the church to become Catharians.

The official position by the Roman church was that these people were heretics and non-Christians and should be wiped out. A crusade was conducted in 1209 that lasted a decade and perhaps a half-million Cathars and Christians were murdered. They ultimately faded out of existence after the fall of Constantinople in 1453 and the remnant may have been absorbed into Islam.

What we learn from the crusades is that the church of the times was powerful, but also intolerant of any whom differed with official Roman Catholic positions. Fear and genocide were weapons of the church late in the Dark Ages and early Medieval Period.

The Inquisitions[13,14,15,16]

When Theodosius made the Christian church the official Church of the Roman Empire in the fourth century, it became powerful, but also rigid. It adopted an attitude of infallibility and the role of sole mediator between God and mankind. It adopted the rules of the faith and also took positions on science that were considered infallible. While various sects of Christianity were declared heretical and the writings and assemblies were banned, not all of them disappeared. Other Christian sects developed over the Middle Ages that differed with Rome. Ultimately emperors and kings, who had been crowned by the Pope, began to reject the concept of coronation by the church. These challenges to authority put the Roman Church in a defensive mode. The church countered with a system of inquisitions, the object of which was to stamp out heresies, protect the power of the church, and keep the masses in strict conformity with its teachings.

A tribunal of Roman clergy would set up shop in a town or city and would publish an edict of grace calling upon any who believed that they might harbor heretical viewpoints to confess. No punishment would be meted to those who confessed. After the grace period any citizens of a town might be called upon to testify and bear witness to any heretical people they might know, including members of their own family or friends. The tribunal would collect evidence and offenders would be brought before at least two witnesses and would be charged with heresy. The accused had no defense counsel, nor could they call defense witnesses. They had to abjure with their hand on a Bible. If they confessed and abjured, their punishment would have been mitigated. If they pleaded innocent or declined to confess they were tortured and then burned at the stake.

The church did not carry out the executions, but delegated that to civil authorities. The church did, however, appropriate the property of those convicted. The process was not democratic, as we know justice today, but one-sided and quite cruel. Had I written this book 800 years ago, I would easily have been a candidate for the stake. So it was in the medieval period that belief in God was not a matter of individual conscience, but obedience to a reign of fear and threat of the instruments of torture.

The Medieval Inquisition

Pope Innocent III started the first Inquisition, called the Medieval Inquisition in 1184, in response to the rise of rival Christian sects such as the Cathars and Waldensians. These movements were popular in southern France and northern Italy. The Papal Inquisitions continued in 1230 by Pope Gregory IX to combat the teachings of the Abilgenses of France. By 1255 the Inquisition was essentially institutionalized throughout Europe, enforced by local Bishops and tribunals, but under the authority of the Pope.

The Spanish Inquisition

The Spanish Inquisition was instituted by King Ferdinand II and Queen Isabella I in 1478 and authorized by Pope Sixtus IV. It targeted converts from Judaism and Islam who were suspected of retaining some practices of their former religions. It also sought

Greek Orthodox Christians.   Essentially this inquisition was developed to protect the state, not the church. It was run by the state, but was equally brutal.   The Spanish Inquisition, as well as the Portuguese Inquisition that followed, were aimed to a large degree toward Sephardic Jews and Moslems who were expelled from Spain.

The Roman Inquisition

The Roman Inquisition paralleled the Spanish and Portuguese inquisitions, but were more in line with defending the faith and assuring that all believers held to the tenets of the church hierarchy. Roman inquisitions continued into the mid-1800s, and even today there remains a body of Cardinals and others who comprise "The Congregation for the Doctrine of the Faith."   Galileo Galilei was caught up in this inquisition in 1633 for arguing and publishing a book that stated that the sun, not the earth, was at the center of our solar system. It took 300 years for the church to officially change its position on the Galileo case.

Protestants were not lily white during these years and afterwards, since they burned more women for being witches than Catholics burned heretics at the stake.

Ostensibly, holy men did very unholy deeds all in the name of God in the Middle Ages and beyond. In hindsight, I consider those deeds as an epidemic of myopia; the result of power, a sense of infallibility, and of a skewed view of reality.

The Reformers

The Reformations, both Protestant and Catholic, primarily came about for two reasons; the first was that abuses by the church were realized; second, that the actions of church of the day were not seen as consistent with the values that Jesus taught. Reformers who saw these improprieties over time spoke out.

John Wycliffe[17]

John Wycliffe was the first of the pre-reformation reformers who stood up against his own Roman Catholic Church. He was born ca,

1324 in Yorkshire, England, and was educated at Oxford where he studied mathematics and the natural sciences, but his driving interest was in philosophy and religion. He received a Bachelor's degree in theology and ultimately a Doctorate in Divinity. He was obviously a brilliant man, well schooled in logic, argumentation, and ecclesiastical law. While Wycliffe was at Oxford, the Black Plague struck England decimating about a third of the population. He was fortunate to have been sheltered in the University and separated from the population at large.

Wycliffe was one of the early reformers in England, two centuries before Martin Luther appeared. Wycliffe and Luther held very similar points of view concerning the wrongs of the church during their times. Wycliffe saw the Roman Church as too powerful and too prosperous. He felt the church should be poor as in apostolic times. He saw a great and unconscionable difference between what the church was and what it should have been. He felt that it was anti-scriptural that Bishops should hold vast amounts of property and wealth. The Bible was the standard of all truth for Christians he maintained. Christ was the Head of the Church, even if in absentia, not the pope.

Over his lifetime he became increasingly adamant about some of his major concerns:
- The right of the state to be separate from the church
- The excess of power and wealth in the church
- The Bible should be the sole authoritative source for faith
- The concept of justification by faith alone

Wycliffe focused on untangling the state from the church. He felt the church did not emulate Jesus' principles. He believed that the church hierarchy was too powerful and too big. He wanted a simpler organizational structure. He was upset by the ostentatious lives the clergy led in England and believed that preachers should live in humility and poverty.

Some of his other reformist views were:
- The concept of transubstantiation in the Eucharist is wrong
- In temporal matters the king is to be above the pope

- He believed that the practice of selling indulgences was wrong
- There was one universal church, outside of which there is no salvation

He believed further that it was proper for the church to pay tribute to the state, as in the days of Christ and the Apostles. He also felt, however, the ruling monarch must wield power in conformity with the laws of God, and that the clergy must be by the Monarch's side to guide him in spiritual wisdom and interpretation.

Wycliffe's later concerns were more theological. He railed against popes who took upon themselves the power to forgive sins and proclaim people doomed to hell or fit for heaven. Instead he saw the Bible being the sole authoritative source for all Christian living. This led him to see that all peoples must be able to read the Bible for themselves. Wycliffe was a prolific writer and produced many tracts and treatises on a variety of topics dealing with the state and theology.

Wycliffe lived during the reigns of Edward III and at the end of his life, Richard II. Edward who reigned 1327-1377 was a good king, loved and respected by his people. Richard II (1377 –1400) was a boy when he came to power, so the throne was really run by his uncle, John of Gaunt who was a supporter of Wycliffe.

When Wycliffe came on the political scene, he felt the church should be poor as the apostles were poor. Both he and Parliament felt that England should not be subject to the rule and tithes imposed by a foreign power (Rome). He opposed church rule over secular affairs. From Wycliffe we inherit the concept of separation of church and state. He believed that those in the church should "render unto the king, that which was due the king," but also that the king had a responsibility to protect the church from all harm and reign in accordance with the laws of God.

Wycliffe also identified with the peasant population, which attended worship to hear the Mass and homily spoken in Latin, a language totally foreign to them. He believed that the people had a right to understand the scriptures in their own language and decide for themselves how they should respond to the gospel. The French had made a translation of the Bible into their language, so Wycliffe decided he would develop a Bible for English speaking people.

In 1382 Wycliffe and some of his followers began the translation of the Bible from the Latin Vulgate into Middle English[18]. There was an early version of the translation that slavishly placed English words where Latin words occurred. This was a mistake because it made the Bible hardly readable. For example, from Wikipedia we read:

Latin words: *Dixitque Deus: Fiat lux, et facta est lux*

Early translation: "And said God: Be made light, and made is light."

A second translation was later made, specifically to make the text more readable. The translation this time would read:

Second translation: "And God said: Light be made, and light was made."

King James Version: "And God said: Let there be light, and there was light."

The translated Bible was widely popular among the people, however the church hierarchy sought to squelch it. The church felt that it alone was capable of interpreting the scriptures and that laypeople had no business trying to understand the scriptures on their own. The translations fulfilled Wycliffe's dream that the laity had a right to interpret scriptures for themselves.

Over his life span Wycliffe went from defending the papacy to wanting it abolished. He felt if the church universal needed a titular head that was okay as long as the right person, ordained by God, was put in the position. Such a pope would be the servant of mankind, not its master. Near the end of his life Wycliffe equated the pope with the Antichrist. Wycliffe also took issue with the monastic orders, saying that the church existed for three centuries without them, and he did not see why they were needed in his day, particularly since they owned considerable property.

John Wycliffe was a thorn in the side of the church hierarchy and through his public statements against the primacy and power of the church, earned him the anger of the popes of his lifetime and after, however he was never excommunicated and died a natural death on December 31, 1384. The Council of Constance held in May 1415 did declare Wycliffe a heretic and decreed that his books be burned. Pope Martin V, in 1327, ordered his remains to be exhumed, burned, and his ashes thrown into the River Swift.

Wycliffe is looked upon as a man ahead of his time. His efforts at reform did not go to the grave with him, but were passed to Jan Hus, the next reformer.

Jan Hus (John Huss)[19,20,21]

John Huss was a Czech born in Bohemia about 1372 and burned at the stake on 6 July 1415. He was educated at the University of Prague and received his MA degree in 1396. He became a lecturer in theology at the university two years later. He was ordained a priest in 1400 and in 1401 he was elevated to Dean of the philosophical faculty.

When Richard II, King of England married Anne of Bohemia, they traveled to Bohemia and brought with them the books and philosophies of John Wycliffe. Huss was greatly influenced by Wycliffe and took up virtually all of his positions on the church. He did not accept Wycliffe's disagreements with the church tenet of transubstantiation of the elements in the Eucharist. That is, the church believed that the bread and wine taken at the Eucharist were miraculously transformed into the actual body and blood of the Christ.

Huss preached to enthusiastic audiences and rewrote many of Wycliffe's works as his own. Huss eschewed preaching in Latin, but rather preached in Czech so that the people could understand him. He was widely accepted because the populace generally agreed that the church was corrupt and pernicious by charging for religious rites and offering indulgences for sale.

As time went on, Huss preached against the sins of the clergy and the errors of the church. About 1408 the archbishop appointed Huss and two others to investigate alleged miracles performed by the blood of Christ in the church at Wilsnack. The group found the claims to be false and deceptive. As a result Huss wrote a tract wherein he encouraged Christians to search the Scriptures and not look for signs and miracles.

Because of his findings, Huss fell into disfavor with the archbishop and he was forbidden to perform his priestly functions within the diocese. The archbishop informed the pope of Huss' actions and his preaching of Wycliffe doctrines so a papal bull was issued in 1409 forbidding the dissemination of any of Wycliffe's philosophies and ordered all of his writings to be burned. The archbishop enforced this bull and 200 volumes of Wycliffe works were burned.

Huss ignored the bull and became bolder in preaching Wycliffe's beliefs. He was excommunicated in 1411 by the archbishop and the city was served with an interdict (all citizens were denied the rites, and they were doomed to hell).

Huss' main beliefs were:

- That the church did not have the right to wage war (Crusades). It was unscriptural as Jesus said to Peter, "Put up your sword."

- Indulgences were wrong, for he said, repentance only, not money, was the basis for the forgiveness of sins.

- The pope does not have the authority to forgive sins, since only God knows who are the elect.

- The church doctrine that the pope's decrees were infallible was blasphemous.

Because of Huss' efforts to reform the church, and his popular backing, there was a lot of strife in the church. The secular and clerical hierarchy both wanted to mitigate this strife. King Sigismund of Hungary decided that a General Council of the church be held to restore peace. The council assembled at Constance and Huss was summoned to appear. He gladly did, knowing that it could be dangerous. The council first addressed Wycliffe's doctrines and found them to be either in error or heretical.

On 5 June 1415 Huss had his first hearing. Articles, which the church deemed heretical, were taken from Huss' writings and charged against him. Some of the charges made against him were trumped up. Witnesses were found to testify against him, but Huss could bring no witnesses in his defense. During the next four weeks of testimony, Huss was asked to recant his beliefs, but he declined. His guilt was essentially foreordained before the trial began, but he was formally declared guilty on 6 July 1415. He was publicly humiliated, stripped of his priestly vestment, and burned at the stake. His ashes were thrown into the Rhine.

Huss defended his beliefs based upon conscience and scripture and not ecclesiastical authority. His martyrdom amounted to ecclesiastical murder. Today the Czech Republic celebrates a holiday in Huss' honor and considers him a national hero.

Martin Luther[22,23]

Martin Luther was born in Eisleben, Germany 10 November 1483 and was programmed by his father to become a lawyer. When he entered law school, he stayed but a short time because he was drawn to theology. Luther wanted certainty in his life and he felt he could better gain this through study of theology rather than law. There was an emptiness in Luther's soul that he need to fill, one that he could fill with study, fasting and prayer. He became a monk and invested himself deeply in his work. He tried to please God through his piety, but that only drove him to understand his sinfulness.

He was ordained to the priesthood in 1507 and began to teach at the University of Wittenberg. In 1512 he was awarded a Doctorate Degree and became a Doctor of the Bible at the same university. Luther's study of the New Testament brought him to understand that justification of people came not from the church, but through faith in God and God's gift of grace. People were justified, not by their works, but only by faith. He further agreed with Wycliffe, that the

Bible was the sole authority for the foundation for the Christian life. Even faith, Luther believed, was a gift from God. Gradually Luther began to see that the church's teaching did not reflect this philosophy.

The Roman church philosophy at the time was that faith alone could not justify man, but only in combination with good works and by donating money to the church. When Rome sent a friar to Germany to sell indulgences to rebuild St. Peter's Basilica, Luther protested. This protest ended up becoming his famous 95 theses that he posted on the Wittenberg Cathedral door, the common bulletin board for the town.

Luther's theses were quickly translated from Latin into German and copies were spread around Europe within weeks. Within months the world knew of Luther. His sentiments were widely popular. Pope Leo X ultimately asked Luther to explain his theses, and after Luther replied, the Pope may have conceded some points, but he did not like the authority of the church to be challenged. In 1520 the Pope gave Luther 60 days within which to recant his views or else he would be excommunicated.

Luther was ordered to appear at the Diet at Worms in 1521 to answer charges of heresy against him and given the opportunity to recant. This he would not do unless his positions could be found to be unscriptural. The church did not take up Luther's challenge so Emperor Charles V declared Luther an outlaw, banning his works and requiring his arrest and or murder by anyone without legal consequence. Frederick III, Elector of Saxony, had Luther spirited to the Wartburg Castle for his own protection and during his fourteen months there he translated the New Testament from Greek into German.

Like Wycliffe's translation for the English people, Luther's translation transformed the German people's understanding of Scripture and helped them understand Luther's theology. Luther's translation ultimately formed the basis of the English King James version published about 1611.

Luther wanted to reform the Catholic Church, but what resulted instead was the Lutheran Protestant church. The Roman church was ultimately embarrassed into stopping the practice of indulgences, but it never admitted any wrong doing, neither did it substantially change its policy of infallibility, nor did it wish to relinquish any power or authority.

Because Luther's philosophies were so popular among the people, the peasants revolted in 1524, not so much against the church hierarchy, but against the feudal power. Unfortunately their anger was carried to extreme and the peasants unleashed many atrocities, all unchristian. Luther sympathized with the peasants but tried to stop this revolt, and ultimately called upon the nobility to squash it. Some peasants did give up their arms in response to Luther, but the revolt petered out against the force of arms. This pent up extremism did find a home with the Anabaptists.

Luther was a petulant Monk, strong-willed and determined, yet pious and faithful to his church. However, he had some leanings we would find distasteful today. He sided with Philip I, Langrave of Hesse, already married, who wanted marry one of his wife's ladies-in-waiting. Luther justified bigamy on the basis that it was practiced in Biblical days. From this we might infer that Luther was a biblical literalist. Second, he was somewhat anti-Semitic. He felt that Christians should be kindly toward Jews, but seek to convert them. When Jews chose to remain faithful to their religion and not take Jesus as the Messiah, he then despised those Jews. He married and approved of priests being family men.

Luther had been in poor health for quite some time and died from heart disease in Eisleben February 18, 1546, three days after preaching his last sermon.

A young colleague, Philip Melanchthon who drafted the Augsburg Confession in 1580, codified Luther's viewpoints. The Confession squarely identified those beliefs that Luther held, and clearly spelled out the heresies of other sects.

Luther wanted the early Protestant Church to maintain some sense of uniformity of liturgy and beliefs and in the main this was achieved. He brought hymns into popular use that congregations could sing. What Luther stamped on this new church was the concept of the

Priesthood of all Believers, and that salvation was the gift of God obtained through belief in Jesus the Christ who was the Hebrew Messiah. Luther's other great gift to mankind was a translation of the New Testament from Greek into German. This led the way for the laity to read the Bible in their own language.

Commoners were eager for any reform they saw because the Roman church raised its wealth and power at their expense. Luther's Reformation spurred other reformers such as Zwingli and Calvin to spread the reformation further. The common people climbed aboard eagerly. Other theological perspectives by these and other reformers brought about the birth of the Baptists, Presbyterians, and through Henry VIII, the Anglican Church.

John Calvin[24,25]

Calvin was a Frenchman, son of the Business Administrator in the Cathedral at Noyon, Picardie, France. He lived 1509 to 1564. His father first wanted him to be a Priest. Calvin was a brilliant and ardent young man, full of religion at a very young age. When his attorney father lost favor with the Cathedral hierarchy, he encouraged his son to study law instead of theology. This, Calvin did. By 1532 he had earned a Doctor of Laws degree. A year or two earlier however, Calvin was struck by a conversion that led him to plunge into Protestant religion with a passion while he completed his law studies. His interest in law waned as a result of his new interest.

Calvin was well educated, very determined, and perhaps bull-headed like Luther in his positions. He studied every nuance of the Bible scrupulously in a very exegetical way, analyzing the scriptures in their original language and in the context of the customs prevalent during the times of the biblical writers. He was perhaps the first theologian to do this. He wrote commentaries on most of the books of the Bible.

He took the Bible literally, and believed everyone should follow what he thought the Bible taught. As such, he organized the Geneva city government to match what was written in the scriptures. That is, there should be four levels of church/city government:

<u>Pastors, or Ministers of the Word</u> - who had authority over all
     religious matters
<u>Doctors/Teachers</u> - who would teach the people
<u>Elders</u> - who would enforce religious behavior on the people and
     also supervise civil activities
<u>Deacons</u> - to minister to the poor, sick, widowed, and elderly.

Implicit in this organization was the fact that church government and civil government were one. It was the practice throughout Europe that a municipality was to be 100 percent of one religion, whether Catholic or Protestant. The ruling Monarch had much to say about which religion his or her nation would follow. France would be Catholic, which is why Calvin ended up in Geneva.

Many Genevans considered Calvin's adamant positions amounted to substituting a Protestant papacy for a Catholic papacy, and they didn't like it. Calvin had to leave Geneva for three years (1538-1541) until a new set of rulers took over Geneva and convinced Calvin to return and reform the church.

Calvin imposed a very strict Bible-based moral code on the populace. Presumably, a moral code was needed. It strikes me that the setup in Geneva was akin to the Sunni Islamic fundamentalist philosophy with the Elders taking a similar, but not as viscous, role in enforcing certain behavior on the people.

Calvin conceived the concept of predestination, wherein God with His foreknowledge knew who would be saved, and actually elected such people without choice on their part being involved. This became the *Doctrine of the Elect.* He further believed that churches should admit for membership only those who were "living saints." Those joining a church would do so of their own free will, but the new church members would agree to behave in a manner consistent with the teachings of Jesus. Calvin believed in an exclusive church. Membership was for the elect, but not for sinners.

Much of Europe followed this rigid and demanding Calvinistic theology. Calvin's legacy to the church today is a democratically managed church and civil organization and the demand for a highly educated clergy.

Calvin was not without his faults however. He tacitly allowed a Genevan opponent (Jacques Gruet) to be tried, tortured and beheaded for threatening him and placing placards castigating his policies. Calvin also wrote the charges of heresy against Michael Servetus, a Spanish physician and theologian, who disagreed with the concept of the Trinity. When Servetus appeared in the church service in Geneva where Calvin was preaching, Calvin saw him and had him arrested. The city Consistory had Servetus tried, convicted and burned at the stake. Calvin did plead to have execution by beheading, but the Consistory was adamant about the more cruel burning.

In defense of Calvin, such practices were common cultural events. Calvin however, did not rise above the cultural practices of the day to raise his voice against such inhuman treatment of people who thought independently and disagreed with official positions taken by Church hierarchy.

To Calvin's credit, his reforms were aimed at improving family life. Men's and women's infidelities were punished equally. Spousal abuse was not tolerated in Geneva because of Calvin. He pushed to improve the life of women and to raise the standards of education and health for all people.

John Knox[26,27]

During the early years of John Calvin and John Knox, Scotland was a poor nation with an uneducated population that was ruled by a wealthy and corrupt Roman church. The church held half the nation's wealth. Morals were in a state of decay. The country was forever at war; either with England or internally with battles among the clans.

John Knox, born between 1505 and 1514 was about the same age as Calvin, born of a farmer, but sent to the university (St. Andrews) to be educated as a priest. Knox was but a young boy when Luther posted his 95 theses to the castle church door in Wittenberg in 1518. By the time he was in the University, the Reformation in Europe was in full swing. By 1540 Knox was a Roman Catholic priest, but he had become a student and supporter of the reformation. Knox obviously was influenced by the martyrdom of Patrick Hamilton, a nobleman and humanist, and Scotland's first reformer who was burned at the stake in 1528 because he had taught reformed theology, which the Archbishop deemed heretical. Knox did not become a parish priest but rather tutored some boys of Scottish noblemen who were sympathetic to the reformation.

George Wishart was a mild-mannered preacher and teacher of the reformed beliefs of Luther and Zwingli. He had been educated at Cambridge in England and in Switzerland and Germany. He firmly believed that salvation came by faith, that scripture was the only standard of truth, that there was no purgatory, and that he was against confession to a priest and the inherent forgiveness by the church. He also felt the Mass as celebrated was idolatrous. He taught his students the scriptures from the original Greek like Calvin, and was accused by Scotch Cardinal Beaton of heresy for his views.

Knox had become Wishart's personal bodyguard and carried a two-handed sword to protect Wishart who had received at least one death threat. The two became very close and Knox was further convinced that Scotland's church and society must be reformed.

Cardinal Beaton had Wishart arrested and he was summarily tried and convicted of heresy and burned at the stake in 1546. The Cardinal was present at the execution. The Cardinal was murdered a few months later by Protestant sympathizers. The sympathizers took over the Cardinal's palace and brought their families and about 150 other sympathizers into the castle for safety. They persuaded Knox to take refuge there also and act as their pastor. This he did.

Mary of Guise, mother to the child Queen Mary Tudor, enlisted a detachment of French soldiers to retake the palace and arrest the inhabitants. As a result Knox and his associates were conscripted as galley slaves. Knox won his release somehow after nineteen months, however his health had deteriorated during this long period at the oars.

By 1549 England was ruled by the boy King Edward VI. The young boy was well schooled and a supporter of the Protestant religion. Knox was licensed to work in the Church of England and given a parish within to minister. He was acclaimed for his skill as a preacher, and he soon was chosen as one of six chaplains to the royal court. In that position, he revised the Book of Common Prayer that Thomas Cranmer had written to reflect more Protestant theology. He worked at court until the 15 year-old king died in 1553.

The Roman Catholic Mary Tudor, daughter of Henry VIII came to the throne. She had Knox exiled to Europe where he met John Calvin in Geneva. There he learned reformed and Presbyterian polity and civic organization from him. Bloody Mary, as she was called, had thousands of Protestants murdered to bring about a reinstatement of the Catholic religion. In the meantime Protestant sympathizers were fleeing England and settling in Germany. Knox took a church in Frankfurt to pastor to the refugees, but didn't stay long because of differences of opinion concerning the liturgy.

After a brief stay in Geneva, he returned to Scotland and continued the Protestant Reformation there in partnership with the Protestant Scottish nobility. He tried unsuccessfully to convince the Regent Queen Mary of Guise to support the reformation. The Roman church Bishops were concerned that they would lose their authority and they summoned Knox to appear before them in a hearing. Knox showed up with so many noble supporters that the Bishops cancelled the hearing. Knox had greater popularity in Scotland than the Queen regent. Ultimately, she abdicated.

Knox accepted one last call to Geneva 1556-1559 immensely enjoying his time there. Meanwhile Elizabeth I became Queen of England. She believed in the freedom of conscience, but also believed the newly reformed church needed the strength and protection of the crown against the on-coming Counter Reformation. From her reign Parliament took over questions concerning the church and state.

Knox came back to Scotland as pastor of St. Giles church in Edinburgh. In 1560, the Scotch Parliament called upon Knox and five other clergymen to draft a new Confession of Faith, which Parliament approved. A year later they approved the Book of Discipline, and the rule that congregations could call their own pastors, but they could not fire a pastor, once called.

Knox wasn't the first of Scotland's reformers, but he was the one who effected the reformation. He brought democracy to the church, and a sense of self-rule. He is considered the father of Presbyterianism and its form of church government originally crafted by Calvin.

The English Church[28]

The Romans had occupied England until 410 A.D. They brought Christianity to England in the third century and it flourished replacing the polytheistic religions that preceded it. The Reformation took place during the reign of Henry VIII who came to power in 1509. Henry was a scholarly and religious man, trained in Latin. He wrote many religious treatises and was acclaimed by the pope as a "Defender of the Faith."

Henry had first married Catherine of Aragon, but the marriage failed to produce a male heir. That brought Henry to become infatuated with Anne Boleyn. He could not divorce Catherine because the Catholic Church did not recognize divorce and to do so would result in his excommunication. Because Henry was desperate for a male heir, he got his lawyers to find a way to dispatch Catherine, while an unknown prelate secretly married him to Anne Boleyn.

Henry's scholarly advisors convinced him that that the Pope's jurisdiction over the English church was false, and that he, Henry, was the head of the church by divine right. Henry was a staunch Catholic and had no doctrinal dispute with the church, but he did not like taking orders from any pope, like many other monarchs.

The Church of England was therefore born with Henry its head. The state immediately appropriated all the property of the church, and Henry had executed two former friends who defied his authority over the church, Sir Thomas More, and Bishop Fisher. The fact that the Pope immediately excommunicated Henry didn't seem to bother him in the least. The Church and the English state were now officially one.

Thomas Cromwell, an intelligent, but ruthless man, became Henry's chief advisor as a member of the Privy Council. Similarly, another friend, Thomas Cranmer was appointed Archbishop of Canterbury.

Cromwell steered the English people toward Protestantism and the first English versions of the Bible translated by Tyndal and Coverdale. In 1538 Cromwell instituted the first system of record keeping of births, marriages and deaths by local parishes. Cranmer, in the meantime, produced the first Book of Common Prayer and the forty-two Articles of Religion for the new Anglican Church.

Because the English church was so closely intertwined with the English throne, it naturally took a course of being regal, stately, and quite formal. That has carried into the American Episcopal Church to a large extent.

The Catholic Reformation[29,30,31]

Protestants call this the Counter-Reformation, but Catholics take the view that reformation had started within the church even before Martin Luther posted his 95 theses. In truth, it might be said that the Catholic Reformation consisted of two parts; the first was a true recognition of problems within the church, the second was a reaffirmation of traditional Catholic theology in reaction to what the church considered was Protestant heresy.

Pope Paul III commissioned a group of Cardinals to form a council and propose reforms within the church. Because there were a lot of intra-church politics involved among Italian, French, and Spanish clerics, the Italians determined that the council be held at Trent in Northern Italy where more Italians could attend than Spanish or French. The Pope called for a council in 1537, but disagreements among the proposed participants forced postponements and location changes until 1545. The German prelates were much more liberal than the Italians and wanted compromise with the Protestants in order to win them back into the fold. The Italians and Spanish were intransigent in their doctrinal views and would not budge.

On matters of reform, there were only minor disagreements among the parties. On matters of theology, there were contentious debates. Because the Italians had stacked the deck by having the greater number of delegates, they won the debate. The Roman Emperor Charles rejected the first report of the Council because of its hard-nosed positions. The Council reconvened in 1551 and in January 1552 a delegation of Protestants was invited to attend.   Neither the Protestants nor the Catholics were excited to be in the company of the other.   Nothing was accomplished by the joint meeting and the permanent divide between the two Christian branches was cemented. A war between Italy and France suspended meetings of the council for 10 years and it did not meet until 1562. The initial meetings were very bitter because the Spanish hated the Roman Curia and wanted to reduce the power of the Pope. The Italians would not accede to the Spanish, so little was accomplished. This was as much a political battle over power than theological.

Pope Pius IV got the delegates back to work in 1563 and the work was finally concluded.

The problems the church recognized and attempted to correct were, in part:

- Its clergy was widely uneducated and without training in Latin, Greek, or theology. The Council ordered that seminaries be constructed in every diocese so that priests could be properly educated.

- Financial abuses, such as the sale of indulgences were acknowledged to be improper. Here the church agreed with Luther. The Italian prelates however made sure that there would be no decline in papal revenues.

- Bishops who were landowners, largely ignored their ecclesiastical responsibilities and to a great extent, spent their time managing their property holdings. Bishops and priests were required to live in their diocese and preach every Sunday and holy day.

- The Bishops could ordain only worthy priests and must discipline those guilty of misconduct.

- The moral behavior of the clergy was tightened and the demand for clergy to live a more ascetic lifestyle was emphasized.

- The streets of Rome were cleared of prostitutes

Doctrinal positions in response to the Protestant Reformation were rigidly held and no compromise was made on any of the Protestant philosophies. The Council held as follows on key issues:

- The veneration of the saints and the Virgin Mary was upheld

- The Latin Vulgate language was declared as Canon and the basis for scriptural interpretation. This elicited much controversy because of the inherent limits of vocabulary in Latin to properly carry exact nuances from the Greek and Hebrew languages.

- Priestly celibacy was reaffirmed

- The doctrine of transubstantiation was reaffirmed

- Salvation was attained by faith AND works, in contrast to the Lutheran/Calvin position of faith alone.

- Pope Pius V arranged that the Roman Missal and Catechism be published and made available to the people.

In addition to these reforms and restatements of the faith, the Popes had officially recognized the Society of Jesus (the Jesuits), which had been formed by St. Ignatius of Loyola. This group of priests and students were dedicated to leading an exemplary life of ascetism and total, uncompromised obedience to the hierarchy of the Vatican. The spirit of the Society could be summed in the thought, "I will believe that the white that I see is black if the hierarchical church so defines it."

As a means of preparing one for obedience to the church, Ignatius' second requirement was that priests learn self-mastery and complete denial of one's feelings or desires. He felt self-denial was a characteristic of a saint.

Their task in society was to educate the masses, fight heresy, and convert the non-believers. The Jesuits were the most successful of the orders, in part because their original leader Ignatius was a former military commander and knew discipline and a military command structure. The Jesuits ultimately became the best educated among the Catholic clergy and naturally fell into the role of seminary instructors and university professors.

Other orders were reconstituted or initiated such as the Carmelites, Barnabites, Theatines, Capuchins, and Ursulines. The Ursulines were dedicated to the education of girls. The Theatine priests were charged with stopping the spread of heresies and to regenerate the clergy. The Capuchins took special interest in the poor and lived ascetic life styles. The Barnabites were also charged with relieving the burdens of the sick and poor and of raising the moral standards of the people.

Further controls by the church on the laity included reactivation of the Inquisitions and the organization of the Index, which was the list of books and publications to be banned and not read by Catholics. The Inquisitions were intended to root out all people who were deemed heretics by the church. Differences of opinion were not tolerated by the Roman church, and to a lesser extent, the newly formed Protestant church. Many people paid the ultimate price for the views they held. Strict, unthinking obedience to authority was the rule of that day, and to a significant extent, that continues in the Catholic faith to this day.

Other Recommendations of the Council

Music in the church was to feature simple melodic lines where words took prominence over the music. Polyphonic music was not to be used. From this the Gregorian chant was made prominent in the Roman worship.

Church facilities were to be made more attractive and inviting to parishioners. This brought about the beautification of cathedrals and churches. The art had to be non-sensuous, dignified, showing the glory of God. Nudity was not allowed. Existing paintings of nude people were to be revised so that nude persons would be modestly draped in clothing or coverings.

The Wars that Followed[32,33,34]

France, Spain, Rome and England were the big players on the political scene in the Middle Ages. The states and religion were intrinsically woven together. Political war became religious war and vice versa. The first battles occurred in France as a civil war between the Guises (See John Knox) who were fanatically Catholic and the Bourbons and Montmorency-Chatillons who were mostly Catholic, but supported the Protestant cause. The French Queen Regent, Catherine de Medicis who wanted to protect her throne for herself and her young son Charles IX, needed the support of the Bourbons, the Montmorency-Chatillons, plus the Huguenots even though they were a small minority in France.

The Guises started the war in 1562 by attacking a Huguenot church and slaughtering all they could catch. After playing both sides against each other, Catherine convinced her son that the Huguenots were plotting his overthrow. In August 1572, the day before St. Bartholomew's Day, royal forces hunted down and executed three thousand Huguenots, and within three days the Guises and the Royal army had executed twenty thousand Huguenots. From that day Protestants started fighting for their own survival. The French wars lasted forty years and thousands were killed.

Phillip II of Spain ruled in the latter half of the sixteenth century. He was fanatically faithful to the Roman Church. He had a powerful military led by his navy. He had stopped the invasion of Europe by the Turks and had started the Spanish Inquisition to rid Spain of Muslim and Jewish converts. He had troops in the Netherlands, which was a Calvinist stronghold. In 1588 his objective was to subdue the Protestants in the Netherlands and move on to conquer England. He built his Spanish Armada for this purpose and armed the ships with 20,000 soldiers. He had another 30,000 in the Netherlands he proposed to pick up. The result was that the English navy, although outmanned, had the longer-range guns and defeated the Spanish by the brilliant tactics of Sir Francis Drake and his colleagues.

The Thirty Years War (1618-1648) was the last major war in Europe, which brought Catholics to fight Lutherans and Calvinists. It was primarily a political war among autonomous city-states, however the city-states each favored a given religion. In the end it became a religious war. It was bloody with untold casualties, but it cemented a great abyss between Catholics and Protestants. After thirty years cooler heads prevailed and a treaty was signed allowing city-states to practice their own religion in relative peace. Out of this, Calvinism was officially recognized in Germany along with Lutheranism.

What Do We Learn from This History

For me, I see that tradition, investiture and power made the church rigid and intransigent. The church was intolerant and change was not welcomed. Second, by having an incestuous relationship with the state, the church gained power and never wished to relinquish it. Tradition caused petrification of dogma, and scriptural interpretation. It changed from wood to stone and was not to be questioned, ever again. Papal authority was unquestionable, and the masses were to be unfailingly obedient to their hierarchical church leaders. The church had become an army of obedient soldiers, never questioning, always obeying.

Like all hierarchical organizations, be they nations, military, or corporations, corruption usually finds its way in. The church strayed quite far from the teachings of Jesus. The Reformation came about because individuals of low rank saw abuses and faults and questioned the church regarding its behavior and its belief system.

This is exactly what I believe laypeople need to be busy at today. It needs to question its faith, not necessarily to take up arms against it, but to see if it makes sense, so that they can honestly own it for themselves.

Why was what people called "heresy" a capital crime? Was it so important that those in power who held inflexible positions be found right? Is this what Jesus taught, be right and kill your opponent if he disagrees with you?

The lust for power was a major reason why people died. That hasn't changed in 3,000 years. Power has no place in religion. Why did Jesus arrive in Jerusalem on a donkey? The people wanted a hero that would overthrow the Romans, but Jesus said, "Render unto Caesar what is his, and render unto God what is His."

Many people in our culture feel the need to be right irrespective of the damage it may inflict on others. The current extreme political rhetoric is an example. This is an ego thing that has nothing to do with issues or truth. If we are declared to be right on a matter by others, we feel good about ourselves. Self-worth comes from within and does not need to come from outside us. When we admit we are wrong, and someone else is right, we can feel good about ourselves. Being open to debate and discussion shows the worth of a person. The outcome of the debate should not matter.

FOOTNOTES

1. Wikipedia, *Manichaeism*
2. Wikipedia, *Zoroastrianism*
3. Wikipedia, *Constantine I and Christianity*
4. Wikipedia, *First Council at Nicaea*
5. mb-soft.com, *Council of Nicaea, Nicea (325)*
6. www.Columbia.edu, *The Council of Nicea*
7. Wikipedia, *Investiture Controversy*
8. www.Medieval Crusades.com, *The Crusades Begin*
9. Wikipedia, *Crusades*
10. Wikipedia, *Muhammad*
11. www.cyberistan.org, *Biography of Prophet Muhammad*
12. Wikipedia, *Catharism*
13. Wikipedia, *Inquisition*
14. www.forham.edu, *Inquisition: Introduction, David Burr*
15. www.etn.com, *The Inquisition, Fr. William G. Most*
16. www.jewishvirtuallibrary.org, *The Inquisition*
17. Wikipedia, *John Wycliffe*
18. Wikipedia, *Wyclif's Bible*
19. Wikipedia, *Jan Hus*
20. www.medievalchurch.org.uk, *John Huss*
21. www.christianitytoday.com, *John Huss*
22. Wikipedia, *Martin Luther*

FOOTNOTES (Con'd)

23. www.wsu.edu, *Martin Luther, Richard Hooker*
24. Wikipedia, *John Calvin*
25. www.wsu.edu, *John Calvin, Richard Hooker*
26. Wikipedia, *John Knox*
27. www.jesus-is-lord.com, *John Knox, The Thundering Scot by Edward Panosian*
28. www.wsu.edu, *Reformation; Protestant England*
29. www.vlib.iue.it/carrie_books, *Chapter 19, The Counter Reformation*
30. Wikipedia, *Counter-Reformation*
31. www.wsu.edu, *Reformation; The Counter-Reformation*
32. www.lepg.org, *The Wars of Religion, Part I*
33. www.lepg.org, *The Wars of Religion, Part II*
34. www.wsu.edu, *Reformation; Religious Wars*

CHAPTER 8

THE QUESTIONS OF FAITH

*In religion we should never go through the motions of reciting creeds
we cannot hold as our own. To reunite the church
we must focus on those core tenets we can agree with and leave aside
that dogma we will never hold in common.*

My Journey

I was asked two questions some years back when I transferred my
membership from one Presbyterian Church to another. The co-pastor
asked me, "Do you take the Bible to be the unerring and authoritative
Word of God, (or something close to that)? "Yup!" I said without
hesitation. "Do you take Jesus Christ to be your Lord and Savior?"
"Yup," I said again. "Next", she said to the next person waiting to be
sworn in, as it were.

I gave the politically correct answers; however today I might take an
hour or more to answer these two questions. This doesn't mean that
my faith is sliding, but my perspective has changed and I hope, for the
better. I reflect on that transaction many years ago, and feel I
answered honestly, but also feel that it was a hollow ritual. I reflect
further that much of what church members recite in worship is done
ritualistically, and that people don't really know what they believe
when they recite in church.

I have been a faithful Christian all my life, albeit, somewhat
ecumenical. I was baptized in a Presbyterian Church, went to Sunday
School in a Baptist Church, was married in a Methodist Church, and
was ordained as an elder in a Presbyterian Church. I've worshipped in
Jewish Temples, Roman Catholic, and conservative churches. I look
at the Bible differently today than as it was presented to me in Sunday
School, and I've learned to experience God differently than the all-
powerful, magical God of my youth. I wish to share with you my
particular spiritual journey, which may very well parallel the journeys
of many other people, both religious and non-religious.

When I was nine-years old and in the fourth grade, I received my first Bible from the Baptist church my parents and I attended at the time. My stern Canadian-born mother immediately sat me down and had me start reading the Bible to her each evening. She unfortunately started with the "Begats" in Matthew (King James version). For a nine year-old, the "Begats" was the wrong place to start. I persevered, very reluctantly, but actually was quite interested to explore on my own this new book I had received.

Even as a nine year-old I began to question what I read. If God made only Adam and Eve, how did the surviving son Cain propagate the race, I thought? Nothing was mentioned about Cain's wife magically appearing. I wondered about the early people living eight or nine hundred years, that didn't ring true even as a fourth grader. Then finally, the miracles of Jesus seemed great, but a little hard to swallow. I thought to myself, "Why was God different back then than He is today?" This was a very natural question based on the contradictions I saw.

Fortunately, I've carried this inquisitive spirit through life, and now have a broader viewpoint on what I had read many years ago. This has led me to write about my current viewpoints on religion and society. I am disappointed that the church universal has mired itself in the past and has relied on pointing to its various scriptures and canons as a basis for supporting very poor social decisions and programs.

American culture, as good as it may be in comparison with other cultures, is based too much on greed, power, violence, play, and ignorance of the needs of the poor and downtrodden. I'm unhappy with what I experience in our society, and don't see our legislative and executive leaders doing anything to change things. I believe the church must step up and influence government and society to reorder its priorities. I do not mean that the church should push a specific religious agenda on society, but rather should guide society to see broader perspectives that provide a win-win situation for all peoples, not just a few.

Where we are Today

I've summarized the evolution of religion in Chapters Four through Seven to show how the church unified, and how it later came apart. In the Hebrew Bible we read about how God interacted with His Chosen People in a very compressed view. Hundreds of years may have passed between God's express interactions with His people. Over the centuries the Hebrews developed their canon. They put together a somewhat legalistic system that included both social and liturgical laws. The foundation of the social law was the Ten Commandments and the wisdom and advice contained in the books of Proverbs and Ecclesiastes. The liturgical canon contained laws on foods, cleansing, sacrifices, and worship. Their Bible also contained history, poetry, wisdom, prophetic writings, miraculous stories, and the Psalms of praise.

The Christian Church evolved from the writings of the early disciples. They wrote and spoke about their experiences with Jesus and whom they thought Jesus was. They agreed that he was the Messiah, the Holy One of God, who came to speak to mankind and save them from eternal separation from God. As the church grew from first-hand knowledge of Jesus and his disciples, differences of opinion arose. The proto-orthodox, the Gnostics, Arians, Ebionites, and the Marcionites all had differences of opinion on who this Jesus was.

Much of this was settled in Nicea in 325 C.E. and some basic core beliefs came out of that Council. However, reformers in the 16th century and popes have divided the church further by additional theological concepts, dogma, and philosophies. Many different expressions of worship have arisen, probably along ethnic and cultural lines, but one major point of division is the interpretation of Scripture. This essentially applies to all religions. One group takes scripture literally as historical fact. The other group takes scripture existentially, taking into account the background out of which the scriptures were written. Both groups take the scriptures to be the authoritative Word of God, but in different ways. This difference of interpretation is the greatest of separators, but hopefully over time, it can be resolved.

That there are differing styles of worship should not bother God at all. He loves the stern Calvinists, the quiet Quakers, the gospel-singing Baptists, the chanting Monks, and the recitatives of the Jewish Cantors equally well, I suspect. Worship style does not separate us.

Theological concepts can separate us, but they should not. I can respect someone else who believes something that I do not. We can both worship the one God who made us both, even though we hold differing opinions and concepts. Differences can be respected, but they should never be separators. As a layperson, I hold some core Christian beliefs that are in common with most other Christians. Some beliefs that others hold, particularly in the Catholic tradition are not significant to my belief system, yet I can still respect my friends from the Catholic, Jewish, Muslim, or Orthodox traditions.

To the non-religious, the church may seem foreign and irrelevant. It's language and hymnody speaks to a culture of many centuries back. The mainline church, in particular, has not created the mountaintop experiences that would convince a non-religious person to become a church-goer.

It may be time for the Christian Church in particular, to redefine those beliefs that are core to its tradition and those that may no longer be core values worthy of dividing us. What are these core beliefs that are essential to lay people and the church in general? We'll review the positions from where we've come and where we need to go to be reunified as a Christian community.

The Mess we're in

Poor Constantine, he rolls in his grave because the church today is as diverse, if not more so, than it was in 325 C.E. Scholars have de-mythologized the Bible to a great extent, and so we pretty well know what is not historical fact. Yet a majority of Christians still hold on to the myths as fact. The myths show God as powerful and magical. Well, God is powerful, and to the Biblical writers and editors, He was magical, and so they expressed their experience in magical terms.

This doesn't work for many of us who do not experience God as performing tricks and arbitrarily controlling nature at His whim. If

He parted seas for the Hebrews, then why does He permit tsunamis, cyclones, and earthquakes to kill thousands? The answer is that God does not abrogate His own laws of nature. He does not cause earthquakes. They are a natural phenomenon of a planet that has tectonic plates that are still moving. Similarly tsunamis, landslides and other soil failures are a natural byproduct of earthquakes. Volcanoes erupt, hurricanes happen, and rivers overflow from heavy rains or abnormal snowmelt. These are the conditions under which we live.

God is not spending His time in heaven looking for bad guys to punish with natural catastrophes. Good people die along with bad people in these events. Abraham had the discussion with God over the good and bad folks in Sodom. Abraham won his argument; the good folks were allowed to escape.

The ancient Jews, and presumably gentiles also, believed that sickness was a punishment from God for some misdeed by the sick person. I think this belief has gone by the wayside. Why then do some people consider natural disasters as a punishment from God? Some of us perhaps, want the bad guys punished, right now, and we're happy to see bad things happen as a means of believing that God is meting out punishment. Surely then logic would have it, that all those people drowned in tsunamis, or children crushed by falling schools must have been bad. This is a set of beliefs that if still held, must be let go.

The Mideastern terrorists declare that they are in a Holy War against the infidels. I believe they must think that anyone who is not one of them is an infidel worthy of being destroyed. They look at the Koran as justification to declare war against Israel for one, and America, for another. I believe that when Muhammad dictated the Koran to his scribe, he referred to Jihad as a war against the Evil One, Satan himself. Mankind's war should be against the Evil One who tries to get us to worship him rather than God. I believe Muhammad wanted to say that Jihad is an internal spiritual war. The meaning of Jihad has been twisted just like the word "device" was used as a euphemism for nuclear bomb. These misperceptions must be let go, because they are wrong.

I've used the term *Myopic Man* as the title of this book to indicate that mankind in general has a shortsighted perspective on life, and religion in particular. I wish to remind people of those factors that make us shortsighted so that we can compensate for them.

As I stand in church and recite various creeds, most of which I can subscribe to, but some statements that I cannot, I feel hypocritical to continue to do this. Why should I lie, particularly in church? I can't lie to God. Then I think back as a pre-teen living with my parents, and listening to my mother decry, "Why don't they do something?" She also would say, "They ought to do something about this." Even as a nine year-old, I would think, "Who are they?" Then I wonder, "How many other laypeople are going through the motions, saying things they either hadn't ever thought about, or that they outright don't believe?" Then I think, "Why don't they do something about this?" Sounds familiar. I know that "they" are preparing for Sunday, or getting ready for their next meeting. Perhaps that is why I'm writing this simple book, to say to myself at least, what I actually believe. I'd like to get somebody else's attention in doing the same thing.

The Differing Views of the Faith

As we read earlier, there were many differences of opinion concerning what new Christians believed and what Jesus' ministry, death and resurrection meant. Just to review what was written earlier:

We understand that the Marcionites believed[1]:
- There were two Gods:
  - One of Creation who was evil and vindictive
  - One of Jesus who was good, merciful and forgiving
- Jesus was divine, but not human, he appeared to be human.
  - This view is called "docetism"
- There was no need to keep Jewish Laws
- Their canon was the Gospel of Luke (minus the first two chapters) and ten letters of Paul
-

The Ebionites believed[2]:
- There was one true God as the Hebrews believed

- Jewish laws must be embraced such that Christianity would be a reformed Jewish religion
- Jesus was the Jewish Messiah
- That Jesus was the most righteous man alive and was "adopted" by God to be His son.
- Jesus was the perfect sacrifice for sin, no further sacrifices were required
- Jesus was not divine, but fully human, the product of the union of Joseph and Mary
- They did not believe in the virgin birth
- They followed the teachings of James, Jesus' brother, who became head of the church of Jerusalem
- Matthew was their preferred gospel

The Gnostics believed[3]:

- There was one true God who created many other gods, one of whom fell from grace and created an evil world as an expression of defiance
- The material earth and all humans (who are material) were inherently evil, trapped in their material body
- Some humans were endowed with a divine spark
- Special knowledge was needed to attain salvation by escaping from the evil body
- The evil creator god required payment for sin
- Jesus was the emissary that brought the special knowledge to earth
- Jesus was a man, but the Christ was a divine creation of the true Jewish God, so he was a lesser God.

The Gnostics were silent about any meaning of the crucifixion of Jesus.

The Proto-Orthodox view[4]:

- Jesus was fully human and fully divine, not begotten, but fully equal with, and of the same substance as God.
- Jesus died for the sins of the world and was raised by God from the dead
- There is a triune God, which includes God the Father, Jesus the Son, and the Holy Spirit

- People needed to believe that Jesus was the promised Jewish Messiah who came to save the people from their sins.
- Christianity was exclusive. One could not worship other gods, only the triune God could be worshipped
- Jesus was born of Mary, a virgin

You can see that there were many contrasting views of Christianity in the first four centuries. Many of Paul's views prevailed. What is the 21st century layman supposed to believe based on further scholarship of the Bible and the context in which it was written? Shall we blindly accept theology as churchmen conceived it 1,700 years ago? Should we go through the motions ascribing to beliefs we never questioned? Should we just throw them out as many have done, or should we study them and decide for ourselves what God reveals to us? There are many mysteries however that I believe can be left as mysteries since they are God's business, not ours.

Roman Catholic Teachings Since Nicea

There are many essential beliefs that the Roman Church and the Protestant Church hold in common, principally, the concept of the Trinity, the Divinity of Christ, Baptism, and the Nicene Creed. As time passed the Christian Church developed finer positions of theology until the period of reformation.   Protestant reformers developed concepts that appealed to the laity and pointed out abuses and weaknesses in the Catholic Church.

The reformers produced new concepts that the Catholic Church could not accept, so the Ecumenical Council of Trent[5] was held during the period 1545 to 1563 both to correct some of the abuses the reformers pointed out, and to affirm the historical teachings of the church and to dispute the positions of the reformers. I'd like to summarize some of the primary teachings of the Catholic Church that include:

- The veneration of Mary and the saints
- The primacy of Peter and succeeding popes
- The infallibility of the pope when speaking ex-cathedra
- The teaching authority of the Church
- Transubstantiation

Mary, the mother of the incarnate and divine Jesus, is referred to within the Catholic community as the Mother of God. As such, she has special veneration for that distinction. Certain dogma has evolved by Catholic scholars over the centuries concerning Mary. I summarize the primary tenets:

- Mary's birth was Immaculate (No male involved)[6]
- She was free from original sin
- She was a virgin when Jesus was delivered[7,8,9,10]
- She was a perpetual virgin, so other children after Jesus were also born of a virgin
- She was taken body and soul into heaven when she died (The Assumption)[11]
- She participates with Jesus in the redemption of souls by her intercession our behalf[12]

I use the writings of Fr. William G. Most to explain as briefly as possible, the basis for the church's belief in the Immaculate Conception of Mary. The church holds that as the future mother of Jesus, Mary was in a state of grace, and as such was free from all original sin and the inclination to sin thereafter in her life. The church refers to Genesis 3:15 and sees a parallel to the mythical Eve and Mary. In this verse God castigates Satan for tempting Eve and the verse reads, *"I will put enmity between you and the woman, and between your seed and her seed; he shall bruise your head, and you shall bruise his heel."* In succeeding verses, God tells of the punishment of Eve and of Adam.

Fr. Most says that if there was to "be complete enmity between the woman and Satan, then she never should have been subject to him even briefly. This implies an Immaculate Conception." Fr. Most also uses Luke 1:28, in which the angel refers to Mary as "full of grace" as a basis of concluding that Mary must have been conceived immaculate. The concept was debated within the church over many centuries, but finally Pope Sixtus IV in 1477 made this concept official dogma. Pope Pius IX in 1854 wrote that God attended Mary from the very beginning of her life, with greater love and gifts than any other human being, and that she was sinless in the sight of God. Therefore an Immaculate Conception was deduced.

Catholic Catechism upholds the concept of the birth of Jesus from Mary, a virgin. It further declares that Mary was a perpetual virgin and that Jesus' younger brothers and sisters, if any, came from miraculous births. The church acknowledges that pagan myths were rife with stories of important figures having been born from virgin mothers and god-fathers. The church takes its basis from Isaiah Ch. 7 and the Gospels of Matthew and Luke. It believes that Jesus' birth was a biological miracle not having a male participant in the conception. It holds that Salvation must come uniquely through Jesus and not through the act of any man.

Fr. Most cites the teaching of the Assumption of the Virgin Mary in excerpts from his Theology 523. In November 1950, Pope Pius XII declared that the Virgin Mary was assumed body and soul into heavenly glory. The church leaves open whether or not Mary actually died or not before her assumption. The logic expressed regarding her death was that if she were free from original sin, she would not be subject to death. The alternate logic was that in her likeness to Jesus who suffered death, she must also have suffered death.

Fr. Most also cites the logic of earlier Catholic scholars that the likeness of the Mother of God and the Divine Son ....forbids the very thought that the Heavenly Queen should be separated from the heavenly King[11]. This thought demands that Mary must not be anywhere but where Christ is.

One last major concept concerning Mary is that she is the conduit, or treasurer, of all grace that flows from Christ the Son. An analogy has been put forth that she is the "neck" connected to the "head", that is Christ, to the "body", which is the church. Using this analogy, the church teaches that all grace flows from Christ through Mary to the church. She therefore, is the mediatrix of the people, to Christ. These concepts began with Pope Leo XIII in 1883 and were carried on by Pope Pius X and succeeding Popes. It was because Mary, as a witness to the crucifixion, suffered, as did her Son, that she merited the position of Mediatrix. The church therefore ascribes to Mary "almost limitless power."

Most of the official dogma concerning Mary came after the Reformation. In any event the reformed church does not take the veneration or the ascribed power of Mary nearly as far as the Catholic Church.

The Primacy of Peter and Succeeding Popes[14,15]

The Catholic Church treats the scripture in Matthew 16:16-18 as the basis for its dogma that Peter was the preferred apostle and the rock upon which Jesus would build His church. In this reference Jesus asked the disciples, *"Who do men say that I am?"* Peter blurted out, *You are the Christ, the Son of the Living God."* Jesus said to Peter that he was blessed, because he learned this, not from others, but only from God Himself. Jesus went on to say, *"You are Peter (Gr. Petra) and upon this rock I will build my church."* This is the famous confession of Peter. A second basis for the church's position comes from John 21:15ff, in which Jesus speaks directly to Peter asking him to *"Feed my lambs."* The church has a strong case for its position, however the Protestant interpretation of the Matthewan text is that the foundation of the church is the confession by Peter of his understanding of whom Jesus was, not Peter himself.

Mark in Chapter 8: 27-30 records the same question, *"Who do men say that I am?"* Peter was the one who answered, *"You are the Christ."* Mark was silent about Jesus' statement about building His church on either Peter or the confession. Luke, in chapter 9:18-21 copied the words from Mark and was silent about Peter. Matthew therefore added the statement about Peter and the rock when he also referred to Mark's gospel. In fairness, Matthew was a disciple; Mark was an eyewitness follower, but Luke was not. Matthew probably had more first-hand accounts with Jesus than did Mark.

Paul, in Ephesians 2:20, writes that the foundation of the church rests on all (twelve) apostles and the prophets before them. He did not single out Peter.

The Catholic Church also takes the Peter and foundation of the church scriptural references to be a basis for implying that there was a hierarchical structure among the disciples, ordained by Jesus, and as a continuance, the Roman church.

According to excerpts taken from *The Primacy of the Pope in the Church* written by Pedro Rodriguez,[14,15] the Bishop of Rome succeeds Peter as the head of the disciples and the church, based on tradition, and the principle of indefectibility and perpetuity of the church. The church further rests its authority in Jesus' statement to Peter that he has given to Peter "the keys of the kingdom of heaven and that whatever he bound on earth would be bound in heaven, and that whatever he loosed on earth would be loosed in heaven." The church assumes its authority and power from this passage, if I have correctly interpreted its writings.

The church also believes that Jesus gave Peter, and his apostles, the power to forgive or to retain sins, and that through succession, the Pope has this right and power. From this, the church assumed its right to issue indulgences.

Infallibility of the Pope[16,17,18]

The church holds that the Pope, as successor to Peter, when he speaks as the official teacher of the faith (ex-cathedra) on matters of faith and morals, is infallible. This is based on three premises:

> 1. From Scripture – that Peter, when given the "keys of the kingdom" spoke infallibly. Through Papal succession, the popes who followed Peter therefore are also infallible when speaking ex-cathedra on matters of faith and morals.
>
> 2. From tradition – Even though the First Vatican Council defined this as dogma in 1870, the church holds that this has always been true.
>
> 3. By logic – The church believes that the Holy Spirit prevents the pope from speaking erroneously, otherwise the " Gates of Hell would have prevailed against the church." Jesus said that the "Gates of Hell" would not prevail against the church.

Infallibility has also been granted to the Bishops of the church when they sit in council together with the pope. This is the Magisterium of the church when the teaching office of the church is gathered together in deliberation on matters of faith and morals.

In the sixteenth century the church felt that it spoke infallibly on all matters including science. That's why they took exception to Galileo's deduction that the sun was the center of our solar system. The church has since quietly backed away from that assertion.

The Teaching Authority of the Church[19]

Fr. Most, writing from the *Basic Catholic Catechism* says "the task of authoritatively interpreting the word of God, whether written or handed on [Scripture or Tradition] has been entrusted <u>exclusively</u> to the living Magisterium of the Church, whose authority is exercised in the name of Jesus Christ." This means that only the pope and/or the bishops in council with the pope may render authoritative interpretations of scripture or tradition.

The writer cites Luke chapter 10 in which Jesus was speaking to the seventy disciples whom He commissioned to go out into the nearby towns and villages in advance of Jesus himself coming and proclaiming the good news. The Church cites verse 16, which reads, *"He who hears you, hears me, and he who rejects you rejects me, and he who rejects me rejects him who sent me"* as the basis of its sole authority.

Transubstantiation [20,21,22,23]

The church believes there is a process of transubstantiation in the Holy Eucharist, which at best, is hard to clearly explain. However, Frank J. Sheed[21], in his *Theology for Beginners*, Chap 18, 1981 explains that the elements of bread and wine have properties of texture, taste, smell, color, etc. When the elements are consecrated by a priest the properties remain the same, but the essential substances of bread and wine change and incorporate the real presence of the body and blood of Jesus. This process is called transubstantiation.

Protestants would teach that in the Eucharist that the spirit of Christ is present as the communicants celebrate together the sacrament of his death and resurrection. The bread and wine are symbolic elements within the reformed church. Catholics teach Jesus is present in the elements. Protestants teach that he is present in the hearts of the people.

There are a number of other Catholic teachings, including the Celibacy of the Priesthood, however I have probably cited the significant teachings that separate the Catholic and Protestant branches of Christianity.

The Catholic Church has put itself in a position where change is difficult, if not almost impossible. It cites its authority from Jesus through Peter to itself. It has justified a hierarchical structure based on Peter (whether self-appointed or Jesus appointed) being the leader of the twelve disciples. It further has delegated all authentic teaching authority in the Roman Pontiff and the Bishops, only when sitting with the pope.   Infallible teachings seemingly are perpetually infallible and may not ever be made fallible. Laypeople are instructed to obey church teachings and not debate them under penalty of anathema. Tradition appears to be as important as scripture. This is a picture of a tight ship.

The Protestant and Anglican Churches were born in rejection to some of these teachings. I expect that an American Catholic church someday may be born in rejection to the unyielding positions the church holds.

The Reformers' Teachings

On matters of faith, the reformers agreed with each other fairly well. Some had opinions on other issues that are not included below.

John Wycliffe
- The Church and State should be separate
- The Bible should be the sole authoritative source for faith
- People are justified by faith alone

John Huss
- Repentance only, was the basis for the forgiveness of sins,
- Indulgences for money were wrong

- The pope does not have the authority to forgive sins, only God, since the pope does not know who are God's elect.
- The doctrine that the pope's decrees were infallible, was blasphemous.

Martin Luther

Luther may have had many more beliefs as cited in his 95 theses, but I present the main points.

- People were justified by faith alone (agreeing with Wycliffe)
- Salvation was the gift of God, as was faith
- The Bible was the sole authority for the foundation of the Christian life (also agreeing with Wycliffe)
- Luther protested the practice of indulgences (agreeing with Huss) essentially agreeing that the church did not have the authority to forgive sins, only God could do that
- Luther believed in the concept of the "priesthood of all believers," which meant that laypeople should be able to read the Bible in their own language and interpret it for themselves with the guidance of the Holy Spirit
- Luther further believed that the laity should hear sermons in their own language, not Latin.
- He believed that priests should be allowed to marry
- He believed in congregational hymns in worship

John Calvin

Calvin was a biblical literalist who believed that both the church and the state should follow the principles laid out in scripture. Calvin's main beliefs were:
- Specification of duties
  - Ministers – Have authority over all religious matters
  - Teachers - Would teach the people
  - Elders   - Should enforce religious behavior, and Supervise civil activities
  - Deacons - Minister to the poor, sick, etc.

- He believed in the unification of church and state (in his day it was the practice that a municipality was one religion or another, never both). His intent was that he wanted the state to function based on moral principles, which only the church could provide.

- The Doctrine of Predestination – God foreordained the elect (God knew in advance who would be saved)
- Church membership was only for the elect, not sinners
- He demanded a highly educated clergy

John Knox
- Developed the Presbyterian style of democratic leadership of the local church, shared by clergy and laypeople
- Accepted the precepts of reformer George Wishart as follows:
  o The church was not authorized to forgive sins
  o Salvation came by faith alone
  o Scripture was the only standard of truth
  o There was no purgatory
- Knox believed in church self-rule, in the Congregational style

I would say that all the reformers believed in the Nicene Creed. All the reformers grew up in the Catholic faith, and at least Luther, wanted to reform the existing church and not start a new one.

Before I get into beliefs different faiths share, foremost in my own mind are a few attributes of God that I hold firmly:

1. There is nothing that God cannot do if He so chooses. Therefore, the church should never issue any dogma that restricts God's potential actions and assign those to itself.

2. God has established laws of nature that allow people to predict the consequences of ignoring those laws. In my experience, God does not abrogate the very laws He created.

3. The creation story in Genesis must be taken for what it is; a story of how early man conceived the universe to have been formed. The story is neither factual nor scientific, but believable by uneducated minds three thousand years ago. I believe that we are in the first hour of the first day of creation that goes on before our very eyes. Stars are being born, elements are being created, and the universe is still expanding. God has allowed mankind to share in his creation by giving us procreative gifts

4. God has given humankind the freedom of choice. We can accept God, or reject Him. The freedom of choice gives meaning to the love that we might share with Him. Similarly, God has the free choice to accept or reject us, as individuals. From this comes the concept of salvation through God's grace. There is nothing we can do to earn God's salvation, it is a gift.

---

5. God is good, beyond our understanding. His love is beyond our comprehension, but there will be a day when the sheep and the goats will be separated. Some will live with Him; others will live out of His presence of their own free choice.

Positions that Christians and Jews share

Christians and Jews can agree that there is one immutable God who created us all in love and made us good. He puts up with our evil ways, but calls us to change from evil and return to righteous behavior. This God follows us and reaches out to us sending us prophets and others to keep us as His people. More could be written, but I stop at the bare essentials. God behaves toward Christians exactly as He does toward Jews. He cares, He reaches out and He gives guidance and wisdom through His chosen individuals.

What separates Jews and Christians is that Jews still await the Messiah. Christians take it on faith that he came in the form of Jesus.

Positions that Protestants and Catholics Hold in Common

Christians start with the Nicene Creed as revised in 381 C.E. much of which, Protestants and Catholics can hold together.

We believe in one God, the Father all governing, creator of all things visible and invisible; and in one Lord Jesus Christ, the Son of God, begotten of the Father as only begotten, that is, from the essence of the Father, God from God, Light from Light, true God from true God, begotten not created, of the same essence as the Father, through whom all things came into being, both in Heaven and in earth; Who for us men and for our salvation came down and was incarnate, becoming human. He suffered and the third day he rose, and ascended into the heavens, and he will come to judge both the living and the dead.
        We believe in the Holy Spirit.

He was crucified for us under Pontius Pilate, and suffered and was buried, and rose the third day, according to the Scriptures, and ascended to heaven, and sits on the right hand of the Father, and will come again with glory to judge the living and the dead. His Kingdom shall have no end.

And we believe in the Holy Spirit, the Lord and life-giver, who proceeds from the Father, who is worshipped and glorified together with the Father and Son, who spoke through the prophets; and in one, holy, catholic, and apostolic church. We confess one baptism for the remission of sins. We look forward to the resurrection of the dead and the life of the world to come. Amen.

I have omitted the concept of the Virgin Mary and Jesus being conceived by the Holy Spirit. Catholic tradition emphasizes this, as do many Protestant denominations. Other Protestants, and perhaps some liberal Catholics do not see this as being fact or necessary for salvation. While God can do anything He chooses, the virgin birth is not consistent with the laws of nature that He developed. Either scenario could be true, but I don't believe the church is in a position to decide one way or another.

Catholics and Protestants share as sacraments, Baptism and the celebration of the Eucharist. Catholics celebrate additional sacraments including; confirmation, Penance and Reconciliation, Anointing of the Sick, Holy Orders, and Matrimony. Anointing of the Sick was at one time referred to as Extreme Unction; an anointing of a person's body with oil, presumably given when the person was in danger of imminent death. Some Protestant groups (esp. Anglicans and Lutherans) also treat Anointing of the Sick as a sacrament.

On Holy Orders there is a variation on a theme. Catholics and Eastern Orthodox treat this (ordination) as a sacrament; Protestants in general, treat ordination as a rite. There are three levels of ordination somewhat common to all faiths:

- Episcopate - Bishops and above
- Presbyterate- Priests, Ministers, and Teachers of the Word
- Diaconate - Elders and Deacons.

In a broad sense, Elders serve the local church Clergy in the running of the church. They participate with the clergy in the distribution of Eucharist elements, religious education, mission activities, and physical plant management. Deacons universally minister to individuals in need.

Apostolic succession is a concept common to both Protestants and Catholics, but in a slightly different sense. This is key in the Catholic philosophy as it is in the Anglican and Orthodox churches. Catholic philosophy is that Cardinals and Bishops follow the long succession of individuals from the apostles and that they share the same ordination by Christ to lead the church. This is not a genealogical lineage by any means, but a spiritual lineage.

Most Protestant churches do not hold this position in the same sense as Catholics do. Protestants do believe that Bishops, ministers, elders, and deacons have been called by God to be ordained to the work that they are commissioned to perform. The rite of laying hands on the head of the person being ordained by previously ordained persons reflects the tradition of apostolic succession.

In the Presbyterian tradition at least, Clergy and Elders are ordained for life. Elders are referred to as Ruling Elders when in office, and Elders when not in office.

It's probably too complicated to describe who recognizes whose ordinations suffice to say that the Roman church does not recognize Protestant ordinations, but does recognize Eastern Orthodox ordinations. Some Protestant denominations are in communion with each other and acknowledge each other's ordinations.

Essential Differences that Divide Us

I will limit myself to those fundamental issues that divide us even if many other less significant polity measures may also add to the separation. Again, I am writing as a layperson, clergy would be quick to point out the issues that I may omit or misinterpret.

Apostolic Succession

Tradition is a major basis for this doctrine. While scripture may also be used, I feel that the interpreter of scripture can make it infer or mean whatever the interpreter wants. This starts in the Roman church with the Primacy of Peter with popes being conceived as a successor to Peter. Protestants, in general, don't agree with this concept, so it is unlikely that this concept will ever be agreed to among Christians.

Restrictive and Exclusive Teaching Authority

The Roman position that the Magisterium is the sole authority to teach and interpret scripture flies in the face of Luther's concept of the Priesthood of all believers. Essentially, Luther was indicating that the Holy Spirit could speak and impart knowledge to anyone God selected. This is in keeping with my point that God can do anything He wants, and the church cannot restrict what God does through His Spirit. Protestants believe that clergy and seminary professors hold a sacred position as Teachers of the Word, but not by exclusive authority, but rather a specification of responsibility.

The Church and the Authority to Forgive Sins

The Roman position is that it has this power as taken from the conversation between Jesus and Peter that Peter would be given the *keys of the kingdom.* The reformers all took the position that only God forgives sin and only He sheds grace upon His elect. The reformers took the practice of indulgences (forgiveness for a price) as a very egregious practice by the Roman church.

The Relationship of Clergy to the People

In my mind, personal relationships fall into two categories; vertical and horizontal. I see the Roman relationship with its parishioners as vertical. This means a relationship akin to Parent-Child or Teacher-Student. While God is the Creator and we are the creatures, I believe that God would like to elevate our standing with Him into a more nearly horizontal relationship. He will always be Creator, and we will always be the creatures, that will never change. As our own children grow and become adults, we as parents can have a horizontal adult-adult relationship with them even though they will always be our children.

Most liberal and evangelical churches hold a horizontal relationship between clergy and laity. The exception would be in charismatic churches where the Pastor can be looked upon as an icon and can easily place himself as the parent of his children. I believe the reformers would see themselves as wanting an adult-adult relationship between clergy and laity even though the clergy had the role of teacher. While we are all branches of the same tree, each of us has different gifts, talents and specialized roles in life. The difference in roles does not make us better or worse than our brothers and sisters.

I suspect that during the first millennium at least, the clergy tended to be educated while the masses were not. That set up a very logical mindset of parent-child relationships within the church. In the twenty-first century, this is no longer true. Lay people are equally as educated as clergy, but with different specialties.

Reading the Bible Literally or Metaphorically

This issue divides churches within Protestant denominations and it can possibly divide liberal and conservative Catholics. As Bishop Gregory Robinson of Australia[24] puts it, there are three levels of understanding scripture:

1. The child-like literal acceptance of Bible stories
2. The metaphorical understanding of Bible stories
3. Understanding the underlying truths that the writers were trying to tell in the literary styles of their day

We would hope that all teachers of the Word would be at level three, however the fact is that some clergy remain at level one. If so, their parishioners are also apt to remain at a literal acceptance of scripture. I tend to believe that even some of the reformers took scripture quite literally and that this literalism became part of the early creeds.

Scholarship in the twentieth century has brought further enlightenment to scripture and Teachers of the Word can better bring parishioners to a deeper understanding of what the Biblical writers were trying to say.

What this division means is that I could never be comfortable in a level one church and it wouldn't matter what denomination it was. Similarly, informed Catholics could not be comfortable in a Catholic church that taught at level one. As laity becomes more aware of scripture and its underlying messages, they will migrate to those congregations that see things at their level.

I suspect that both Luther and Calvin may have understood the Bible literally. The growth of seminaries and the intense study and discussion among theologians of all faiths has led to a deeper understanding of scripture during the last fifty years.

Investiture in a Hierarchy

Wealth and power go together. Jesus commented to the disciples after the rich young ruler asked him about what he had to do to gain eternal life, *"It is easier for a camel to go through the needle's eye than for a rich man to enter the kingdom of heaven."* The needle's eye, I was told, was a narrow slot in the Jerusalem wall that people could get through as a short cut, but it was a very tight squeeze for a camel.

There is corporate power, political power, military rank, and religious power. Almost universally, those in power do not voluntarily relinquish it. The point is that those in power often become invested in that power and are loathe to surrender it. The church also falls into this position. The Roman Church has a hierarchy, and with it, liturgical power, and I feel it will never surrender it even for its own good.

Jesus sent the seventy disciples into the field with absolutely nothing except what was on their backs. They had to trust in God's power, not their own. So it is with the church, the church will gain its strength from its weakness. Religion is about trust and obedience, not power.

The Key Questions of the Faith

If you are a layperson, what do you believe? How far do you carry your beliefs? Is there a vast array of things you believe about faith, or just a few core beliefs? Possibly you believe what you were taught or told to believe. Casting aside past teachings, what do you believe today, whether Christian or not? I've asked myself these questions and you can see how I approached the questions in preparing this book. We, together, are certainly biased by our backgrounds and culture and many of those other constraints I listed in Chapter One. Basically, I believe we should be guided by our personal experience with God. I am also guided by what I observe in nature, because there, we see the handiwork of God.

I've put together a list of topics that I have thought about. You may have more, and if so, go at them. There are probably many questions that could be listed pertaining to the faith, but I will list only those that I feel are significant. These are:

- Is there original sin because of the disobedience of Adam?
- Should the Hebrew Testament miracles be taken literally?
- Does God require payment for sin?

- Does sin require a payment of death? If so, what is the nature of that death?
- Were there an immaculate conception and a virgin birth?
- Did Jesus and the Apostles really perform miracles?
- Was Jesus God, like God, human, or both God and human?
- Is Christianity the exclusive means to salvation?
- Was Jesus physically resurrected?
- Will there be a Judgment Day?

I probe these questions below. The answer to most of the questions I have raised is; "I don't know." However, I answer them in the context of my own personal experience of the God that I know loves His creation and me. I encourage readers to take this same gamble. If life is a pass-fail test, I feel most of us are in trouble. However, not to take the test is a cop-out. I want to stand in church and proclaim what I can own as my personal beliefs, right or wrong. I think this is what God wants us all to do.

Keep in mind that God is not proposing that we take an exam to enjoy paradise, but just to trust and obey Him.

Original Sin

The Bible reads that Adam and Eve were disobedient in the Garden. They ate the apple when they were told not to. It's all their fault. Well, there was no Adam and Eve, and there was no Garden, but there was a Biblical writer who felt he had to explain why there was sin in the world. He pinned it back to the beginning. I expect the cavemen sinned. They fought with each other, and probably killed those whom they regarded as threats or enemies. They lived with constant fear. This was part of the defense mechanism that kept them alive and that we are all born with.

Does a newborn baby get delivered from its mother's body as a sinner? I don't think so. This young object of love hasn't had time to even know what evil is. This young baby is good, not evil. The baby is a product of God's creation that He made good. God shared the ability to create with men and women, that they might know the goodness of creation. The Evil One inevitably will attack any young child at some point, but the child was not born with a tag on its toe reading, "Original Sinner." The child was not inherently evil the child was inherently good. God's creation was inherently good, He does not create evil.

The Evil One is always looking for converts so that he may gain power. He will invade the human soul at some point early in our lives with temptations and clouding our reality. In this respect, there is the <u>inevitability</u> of temptation and sin. All of us easily fall victim to the Evil One. The Holy Spirit, however, gives us courage, clear vision and incentive to remain righteous.

As children grow and develop in their teenage years, they do things that irritate their parents no end. They do things not in their own best interest. Young people don't see themselves as their parents do. They fail to predict the consequences of their actions. Parents worry that they may kill themselves by driving too fast, showing off as it were to others in their cars. They <u>inevitably</u> mess up.

So it is with God. He sees us doing things that are not in our best and long-term interest. He worries about us because He wants us to grow up and enjoy eternity with Him.

Sin is the product of the Tempter clouding the perceptions of any human, and that human accepting the misperception and consequently acting out an evil in disobedience to the Holy Spirit, who is providing advice contrary to the Evil One. Yes, we are all sinners as Paul wrote, but God has given us the freedom of choice to obey Him or obey the Evil One. We are never without choices, in my opinion. Jesus was tempted, not just in three scriptural instances over 40 days, but over His entire, short life. He chose to be sinless as a human being. He chose to be obedient, even to the point of losing His life for His obedience.

Evil is the product of two elements, neither of which is genetics. The first is myopia, a lack of seeing things clearly or objectively. It is a product of ignoring reality and painting a situation with a cloak that covers reality and is pleasing to the viewer. The second is disobedience. It is the choice to act in self-interest to the disadvantage of another. Evil is the failure to love.

Sin comes early, and to all of us, but we can't blame the mythical Adam or God. I don't believe sin was original because God did not originate it. Sin, to me, is not original it is rather, <u>inevitable</u>.

Should the Hebrew Testament Miracles be taken literally?

My personal, and limited experience and understanding of God is that He created the universe and the laws of nature, and does not abrogate those laws. God does not turn gravity on and off at a whim to cause a miracle to happen. The statement that if we had sufficient faith, we could move mountains to me was not to be taken literally, but figuratively. Were the plagues cast upon Pharaoh and the Egyptian people before the Exodus the magical works of God? Of course not. They happened and were written about many years after the fact, but in context of what happened, the Exodus writer ascribed them to be the wondrous acts of God. This was a belief of the Hebrew people, that God rescued them. The Red Sea was not parted as Cecil B. DeMille portrayed in his movie, the *Ten Commandments,* yet the Hebrews did get through the shallows, as most scholars believe.

The culture of the day was to heighten heroes by writing in miraculous terms. This trend carried over into New Testament writings as well. It was a cultural norm. The point is not to get focused on the violation of the laws of nature, but rather to see the picture the writer was trying to paint. The proto-orthodox view was to read scriptures first literally, then figuratively.

Sacrifice and Atonement

As Bart Ehrman has said in his lectures, people in biblical times lived on the edge. They were totally dependent on the herds for meat, milk, and hides. They were dependent on the weather for the growth of their crops. They also needed protection from marauding tribes and bandits as well as wild animals. They lived in constant uncertainty, regardless of where in the world they lived. Early mankind believed there was a power higher than them upon whom they relied for their survival. From this they believed that they had to please this, or these, unseen higher beings. The concept of sacrifice arose among all peoples, not just among the Hebrew people. An unwritten deal or covenant was conceived. If you provide for us and protect us, we'll worship you and sacrifice to you. We will do what it takes to please you. The smoke from our sacrifices will rise into the heavens, and the odors should please you. This was the mentality of mankind from the period from Noah to Christ.

Keep in mind that the early concept of the universe was that it consisted of three tiers; the flat earth, the heavens and stars in the dome above, and Sheol below. Ancient people believed the gods were close and that they could physically smell the odors of their sacrifices.

I look upon the mentality of sacrifice as akin to the political act of bribery. Mankind was trying to manipulate the gods into caring for them. The act of manipulating the Living God would be an offense and insult to Him. God cares for His people without their knowing it. He neither slumbers nor sleeps, and is aware of each creature by name. God is interested in our love as a free choice by us. We love God by loving others. We love God by being just and kind to others. He is not interested in smoke rising from sacrifices, neither in blood being shed for His benefit. I suspect He viewed Mayan vestal virgin sacrifices as abhorrent.

Out of this mentality Jesus became perceived as a sacrifice like the pure, unblemished Hebrew lambs. The analogy would be immediately obvious to the Jews in the time of Christ. Liturgical sacrifices were an integral part of Jewish law. The specifications were clear and strict about sacrifices. The Levitican rules were exacting, but what was it that God really wanted. Animal sacrifices were a practical way for a nomadic tribe to express appreciation to God. I suspect however, that what God wanted was a product of the hearts of people, not of the smoke from baking lamb. He wanted devotion in the form of faith in Him, and obedience to His will. He wanted people to love and honor each other and to treat each other with dignity.

So was Jesus a sacrificial lamb who died as a payment of a ransom for all? This has been a standard evangelical statement for 2,000 years. In my understanding of God, I have some problems with this symbolism. To whom was a ransom being paid? Was it to God or the Evil One? Did God really want a blood sacrifice like the Mayan's offered? It doesn't make sense to me. Does God have bookkeepers in Heaven jotting down every sinful debt we have taken from Him? This is not my concept of the Living God. He is not a Scrooge with a thick ledger containing the debts of all who owe him.

John had it right in chapter 3, verse 16; *"God so loved the world, that He gave His only begotten Son...."* Jesus death was an extreme act of love on God's part reaching out to us to show us that we must be like innocent lambs before Him and that we must be obedient to His will for our own spiritual good. If we are to have a relationship with the perfect God, we must be perfect like Him. Jesus' death has symbolically erased our past and future sins, so we can be accepted by God as we are.

If there was a ransom to be paid, it went to the Evil One, not to God. It went to remove the power of the Evil One to prevent God's people from having a loving relationship with Him. For me, the concept of a debt paid is not what I feel; it is more the extent to which God has reached out to us to win our loyalty to Him. I see a different emphasis, not of a God expecting payment, but of a God reaching out. There is a big difference in these two concepts.

Jesus had to die for God to show that there would be a resurrection. I do believe that Jesus actually appeared to the disciples after his death, but whether He literally ascended into the sky in their view, I don't know. I trust that He returned to the Father by whatever means. I do understand that whatever happened, the disciples knew that Jesus was alive in spiritual form and communicated with them in such a way that their breath was taken away. They had to have been overwhelmed by this experience to do the things they did in their missionary journeys.

God had not demonstrated the concept of resurrection to the earlier prophets. It was sufficient to show the Hebrews the Laws of behavior that God expected them to follow and for the path He had expected them to walk.

Does Sin Require a Payment of Death?

I believe the word 'require" is the wrong word in this question. Spiritual death is the natural result of sin. God will not live in the presence of sin. It would be a contradiction in terms. God is Love and those that have an intimate relationship with Him, must be sinless also. Death, to me doesn't imply the physical death we experience on earth, but rather an eternal separation from God. That is worse than death, because it is forever. So, if I were to rewrite this phrase from Paul (i.e. *"The Wages of Sin is Death"*), I would say that the result of sin is, *"Eternal separation from God."*

The Virgin Birth

Like most scholars, I understand the concept of the virgin birth as a myth common to many notable people in ancient times. It was a cultural understanding ascribed to emperors, heroes and unique leaders of the day. That Jesus would not have been born of a virgin does not diminish God's act to rescue mankind through Jesus. The fact does not diminish my faith. The Bible is full of miracles from beginning to end. It was the custom of the day to ascribe miracles to notable people. Jesus was no exception. Christians won many converts from paganism because Christians would claim the miraculous powers of their God. The argument for conversion was that the Christian God was more powerful than any man-made god.

The proto-orthodox people of the period, I'm sure, leaned on the Gospel of Matthew in which every Hebrew Testament prophecy was projected onto Jesus as a fulfillment. The virgin birth statement in Isaiah 7:14 was used by Matthew in 1:23 to demonstrate a fulfillment by God.

There are reasons why religious people would stand by a literal interpretation of a virgin birth, because it could be said that salvation came by no act of man. Our experience on earth tells us that virgin births do not occur, and that God does not annul his own laws of creation. We don't need to have a virgin birth to have a vital and realistic faith in the act of God. Therefore, in disagreement with orthodox statements, I subscribe to neither an Immaculate Conception, nor a virgin birth, neither changes my faith, and my disbelief is consistent with my understanding of God working in this world.

Did Jesus and the Apostles Really Perform Miracles?

What Jesus and Apostles did may have been miraculous, but they did not perform miracles in the sense that the laws of nature were abridged. The New Testament as well as the Hebrew Testament is full of legendary statements. These miracles are part of that practice. This does not make the Scriptures invalid, or faith in Jesus a waste. The miracles were literary practice of the times that represented indescribable events. The divine Jesus was also fully human, and so existed within all the limitations we have as human beings. He did not turn his divine powers on and off as He chose.

Was Jesus Divine?

Better men than I certainly wrestled with question for the first three centuries. The Ebionites said he was God, the Marcionites said he was human, but not God. The Proto-orthodox said he was both God and human, and that's where we are today. Assuming none of us had heard these previous views, what would we say based on the scriptures, which is all we have to judge from? We must search for the clues from what Jesus said about himself. He certainly pointed to the Father in Heaven implying a spiritual relationship. For example in Matthew and Mark:

Mt 3:16, Mk 1:10 Lk 3:22 When Jesus asked John to baptize him, John argued that Jesus should baptize him, but Jesus prevailed, and immediately upon the completion of the baptism according to the gospels, the heavens opened, and The Spirit of God like a dove descended upon Jesus, and the voice of God was heard to say, *"This is my beloved Son, with whom I am well pleased."*

Mt 5:15 *Let your light shine ...that they may see your good works and give glory to your Father who is in Heaven.* This was a saying of Jesus.

Mt 12:17 Matthew writing about Jesus having healed the man with the withered hand and many others said, "This was to fulfill what was spoken by the prophet Isaiah: *Behold my servant whom I have chosen, my beloved with whom my soul is well pleased. I will put my spirit upon him, and he shall proclaim justice to the gentiles…"* Mark wrote about the healing in 3:1, but was silent about the saying that Matthew added.

Mt 16:13 Jesus asked the disciples, Who do men say that the Son of Man is? They answered; some say John the Baptist, others say Elijah or Jeremiah or one of the prophets. Jesus asked, who do you say that I am? Peter said, *"You are the Christ, the Son of the Living God."* Jesus, confirming that Peter was correct said, *"flesh and blood has not revealed this to you, but my Father who is in heaven."*

In this scripture, Jesus confirms that he is the Messiah. He also goes on to indicate that he will build his church on Peter (also indicating, because of the play on words about Peter being a rock) that his church was also being built on Peter's understanding (confession) that Jesus was the Messiah. Without getting caught up on the confession, it might be more nearly correct to say that the church is built on understanding whom Jesus is.

Mt 20:22 When the mother of James and John, the sons of Zebedee asked Jesus if her sons could sit on thrones adjacent to Jesus when his kingdom came, Jesus essentially answered, *You don't know what you are asking for."* *"Can your sons go through the agony I will go through?"* She said yes, but Jesus indicated, *"it is not for me to grant to whomever shall sit on my left and right, that is for my Father in heaven to grant."*

Mt 24:36 Jesus was talking about the apocalypse and the signs of the end of earthly life, but he said, *"But of that day and hour no one knows, not even the angels, nor the Son, but the Father only."*

Mt 25:31 Jesus said, *"When the Son of Man comes in his glory, and all the angels with him, then he will sit on his glorious throne."*

Mk. 14:62 Jesus at his trial was asked by the Chief Priest, "are you the Christ (Messiah), Son of the Blessed One?" Jesus said; *"I am; and you will see the Son of Man seated at the right Hand of Power, and coming with the clouds of Heaven."* Matthew does not have Jesus answer the Chief Priest (Mt 27:14), but he remains silent. When asked a similar question by Pilate (the Governor), Jesus responded, *"You have said so."* Luke in 21:27 also speaks of Jesus coming with the clouds of Heaven, copying Mark.

Luke wrote of Jesus (26:67) when he was on trial at the high priest's home, was asked, "If you are the Christ, tell us." Jesus said, *"If I tell you, you will not believe".....But from now on the Son of Man shall be seated at the right hand of the Power of God."*

It is in the gospel of John that the writer says that *"Jesus was the Word, and that the Word was with God, and the Word was God. He was in the beginning with God, and all things were made by him…"*

Jn 4:26 Jesus first reveals himself to the Samaritan woman at Jacob's well in Sychar, Samaria when she said "I know that the Messiah is Coming." Jesus replied, *"I who speak to you am he."*

Jn 5:19 Jesus said of himself, *"The Son can do nothing of his own accord, but only what he sees the Father doing; for whatever He does, the son does likewise."*

Jn 5:30 Jesus goes on to say, *I can do nothing on my own authority; as I hear, I judge; and my judgment is just, because I seek not my own will, but the will of him who sent me."*

Jn 14:11 Jesus said, when answering Philip's request to show us the Father; *"He who has seen me has seen the Father." I am in the Father and the Father in me."*

Essentially, this is the evidence we have to make a decision on the divinity of Jesus. If we take the miracle healings literally, then there would be no question of Jesus' divinity. If we conclude however, that these were miraculous stories about Jesus and that they should not be taken literally, then the problem is harder.

John states that Jesus and the Father were One, and that they were together in the beginning. The three other disciples did not express themselves that way. They indicate a Father-Son relationship in which God poured out his spirit upon Jesus at his baptism. When

God poured out His Spirit upon Jesus, he acquired the spiritual substance of God. They were of one substance. When Jesus was brought to the Temple in Jerusalem as an infant for his parents to make a sacrifice, Simeon, who was guided by the Spirit to come and see Jesus, acknowledged that Jesus was to be the salvation for the Jews and Gentiles.

Jesus himself indicated that He would come in glory with His angels at the apocalypse and that he would sit at the right hand of the Power of God. Jesus also indicates in John that his work on earth is on the authority and wisdom of the Father. He does nothing on his own accord.

These statements are sufficient to convince me that Jesus was divine, but that he was begotten of Joseph and Mary in fully human form, and given divine status by God. Even as an earthly father and son have the same DNA and similar genes, they are alike, but different. I have to side with the orthodox, that Jesus was fully human and his personality was filled with the spirit of God. Jesus always spoke to God as a Father, indicating he respected God as the higher authority, and that His Father gave authority to him. Logically, I must disagree with the author of the Gospel of John. If Jesus was God from the beginning, it wouldn't make sense, by current Western thought, that God would then pour out his spirit on Jesus. That spirit would already have been there.

Right or wrong, it doesn't change the fact that God reached out to the Jews and Gentiles through His divine son Jesus to offer salvation to the world. Jesus was the Messiah and he brought the knowledge that would allow mankind to live in peace and love and the fullness that God intended.

Is Christianity the Exclusive Means to Salvation?

I would suspect that most Fundamentalists and Evangelicals would answer, yes. Again, I must look for the evidence. I start with the book of John. Nicodemus asked Jesus how one could be saved? Jesus replied, *"by being born again."* Nicodemus then asked how that could be done. Jesus again replied, *that unless one is born of water and the spirit, he cannot enter the kingdom of God.* The water that Jesus speaks of is not literally water, but life-giving wisdom that Jesus taught as he discussed with the Samaritan woman at Jacob's well. The water was the Word of God.

The Spirit that comes to men and women is like the wind, we hear it, but do not see it or know its origin. Jesus implied that the change in the spirit of men and women is a gift to an open heart. He went on to write in Jn 3:16 *That whosoever believes in his Son, should not perish, but have everlasting life.*

Here we all must step back and see the context in which the gospel writers expressed their experiences. Jesus was their entire life for the length of Jesus' ministry, probably a couple of years. He was everything. The gospel writers were expressing their emotional experiences. They were not giving an academic exposition on the means of salvation. That's not where their heads and hearts were.

Jesus again says in John 5:21 that the Father has given all judgment to the Son, so that the Son will give life to whom he will. He goes on further to say (5:28,29) that those who are in their tombs will hear his voice and rise to judgment according to their deeds. To me this indicates that eternal life is not restricted to Christians, nor those Christians of any given faith or denomination that believe they have the only answer. God is not exclusive. He wants all who choose to come to Him, to do so according to their belief in Jesus, or failing knowledge of him, to their faith in God and their love for their fellow men.

I do not believe that God is impressed by mechanical or legalistic worship of Him. He wants people to be sinless, but He understands our difficulty in achieving that goal. He asks to be loved, and He asks that we love our neighbors. Terrorists who kill in the name of Allah do not meet the criteria of loving their neighbors. Nonetheless, God wants Muslims, Buddhists, Jews, Christians, agnostics, Gays and Lesbians, who love him and love their neighbors to have eternal life. Jesus is to be the judge of that.

Is Christianity the exclusive means to salvation? The answer must be, "no!"

Was Jesus Physically Resurrected?

From what I have read, scholars have differing opinions on this question. I tend to agree that the burial by Joseph of Arimathea may have been concocted to allow an Easter morning empty tomb scene. Dominic Crossan believes, if I understand him correctly, that Jesus body probably was left on the cross to be scavenged by wild dogs and animals. Nevertheless, without a physical resurrection, the purpose of the gospels would have been empty.

The resurrection of Jesus would have been the one event where God physically acted in the world to perform what we would call a miracle. We take the resurrection on faith. The gospel writers testified to having seen, talked and eaten with the resurrected Jesus. I can't believe they made this up. Mankind will surely experience a resurrection even as Jesus experienced. He said to the criminal on the adjacent cross that this day he should be with me in paradise. Jesus was indicating that physical death did not mean death of the soul. Death was a portal to be passed through. The resurrection would be a final step. So, yes I do believe there was a physical resurrection of Jesus.

Will There be a Judgment Day?

When I start to think about this, I am immediately reminded of the parable of the talents. To one was given three, to another two, and to the last, one was given. The first two returned interest on their gifts, but the last one was afraid to lose what he was given and so didn't invest his talent. The donor of the talents took away the sole talent from the last and gave it to one who had more. The point was, that there was an accounting. At some point we must account for the gifts we are given.

I can't quite see myself in a great hall or field with 10 or 20 billion other people lined up waiting to face Jesus. That would not be a comfortable situation. Since my last name starts with a "W," I perceive I'd be in the back of the line. I do not see a vengeful God, but I understand a just God. Mankind brings his or her own judgment upon himself or herself. I suspect we would all flunk the test if it were based on goodness alone. We will account, but grace will cover the failing grades.

The victims of persecution will have their day in court, and they shall see their persecutors punished. There shall be great sorrow that day, but there shall also be rejoicing.

How Do I differ from the Council at Nicea?

The issues I differ with the church fathers of 381 are; the virgin birth, conceived by the Holy Spirit, laying the responsibility of all of Jesus' suffering on Pontius Pilate, and finally, whether Jesus was present with God before all time.

Neither the Immaculate Conception of Mary nor the virgin birth of Jesus are beliefs that I feel are essential for salvation. That Jesus was the Messiah is essential and that He is divine is essential.

Pilate, as Roman Governor was in place to keep order and protect the eastern flank of the Roman Empire. It was his job to remove any threat to the empire. Jesus claimed only to be king of the Jews, and Pilate seemed to feel he was not a threat to the Empire, otherwise he would not have offered to let him go. The temple establishment, however, did not want their position compromised by Jesus. They set up false witnesses to yell for the release of Barabas, a known desperado. Pilate did cave in to the pressure, but both the religious establishment of the day and the Roman chief, must share the immediate responsibility for Jesus' suffering. Mankind in general, must also be responsible for his death because of its unbelief.

Whether the Trinity existed from all time, I don't know. Certainly, the substance of God, which also comprises Jesus and the Holy Spirit has existed from all time. Jesus acknowledges that the Father knows things that he, Jesus, does not. He implies that he has a personality separate from the Father, but of equal spiritual substance and quality.

I did not see evidence of this issue in the Scriptures, but neither was it a legalistic issue with me. I am comfortable with the mystery and don't need the answer.

The virgin birth is a carryover from Hebrew scripture and Mideastern culture of the period. The divinity of Christ, the concepts of the trinity and the resurrection I agree with.

These are the things I believe. I am certainly influenced by my education, upbringing in church, and I am aware that I cannot see things clearly. Yet, with all my constraints, I have interpreted from Scripture and my experience, those things that I believe. If I were a law-abiding Catholic, I should not have done this. I have felt, however, that I must be responsible for my own beliefs, so I have laid them out for you to see and to ponder for yourself. I encourage you to make your own journey. It may be different from mine, but I would take it to be equally valid.

We've looked back on the church. Ahead I'd like to compare the collapse of the Roman Empire with the precarious position the American Empire has placed itself. I see the need for reform of the American culture and world behavior. I believe only a united church can bring about reform in the world, specifically, America first. I believe unification can and must be achieved to save our nation.

FOOTNOTES

1. Ehrman, Dr. Bart D., *Lost Christianities, DVD Lecture 3*
   The Teaching Company
2. Ehrman, Dr. Bart D., *Lost Christianities, DVD Lecture 2*
   The Teaching Company
3. Ehrman, Dr. Bart D., *Lost Christianities, DVD Lectures 4,5, &6*
   The Teaching Company
4. Ehrman, Dr. Bart D., *Lost Christianities, DVD Lectures 20-24*
   The Teaching Company
5. Wikipedia, *Council of Trent*
6. Most, Fr. William G., *Mary's Immaculate Conception,*
   www.ewtn.org, online
7. Bennet, Jonathan, *The Catholic Understanding of the Virgin Birth,*
   www.ancient-future.net, online
8. Rhys, Jocelyn, *Shaken Creeds: The Virgin Birth Doctrine 1922*
   www.englichatheist.org, online
9. Wikipedia, *Virgin birth (mythology)*

FOOTNOTES (Con'd)

10. Ontario Consultants on Religious Tolerance, *The virgin birth (conception) of Jesus,* www.religioustolerance.org online

11. Most, Fr. William G., *The Assumption of Mary into Heaven* www.ewtn.com, online

12. Most, Fr. William G., *Church Teaching on Mary as Mediatrix of (All) Graces,* www.ewtn.com, online

13. Most, Fr. William G., *Mary's Cooperation in the Redemption* www.ewtn.com, online

14. Rodriguez, Pedro, *The Papacy and the Primacy of Peter, Part 1,* www.ewtn.com,

15. Rodriguez, Pedro, *The Papacy and the Primacy of Peter, Part 2,* www.ewtn.com

16. Mirus, Jeffrey, PhD., *Papal Infallibility,* www.ewtn.com, online

17. Wikipedia, *Papal Infallibility*

18. The Catholic Encyclopedia, *Infallibility,* www.newadvent.org, online

19. Most, Fr. William G., *The Magisterium or Teaching Authority of the Church,* www.ewtn.com, online

20. Wikipedia, *Sacraments of the Catholic Church*

21. Sheed, Frank J. *Transubstantiation,* www.ewtn.com, online

22. www.allsands.com, *What is Transubstantiation?*

23. www.evangelicaloutreach.org, *The Present-Day Official Teachings of the Roman Catholic Church*

24. Robinson, Bishop Geoffrey, *Confronting Power and Sex in the Catholic Church, 2007*

CHAPTER 9

BUILDING A UNITED CHURCH

The Status of the Church Today

As a layperson, I see the church in transition. Many congregations are shedding their denominational identification and many others are independent. Congregations are small, competitive, and passive. I see part of it out of touch with society, cloistered away in hallowed sanctuaries, preaching to the choir. All this needs to change. Jesus sent his seventy disciples out into the hillsides to convert the Gentiles encouraging them to do miracles in the face of certain hostility. Today's church could also do miracles if it willed itself to do so.

Few members join a church from a theological basis alone. For example, few people who attend Presbyterian churches join because they fully agree with the teachings of John Calvin or John Knox. They may or may not even know who these men were and what they stood for. If they knew Calvin they may agree with his principle of democratic rule within the church, but may disagree with his idea of predestination. Calvin today probably wouldn't be a Presbyterian. He might be a conservative Southern Baptist perhaps, or possibly a Quaker. I see him as being against gay rights and having a viewpoint on whom should be welcomed into an exclusive church.

Laypeople look for churches that are socially active and can provide nurturing for their children. Others join because its leader is charismatic; still others look for a certain style of worship, whether traditional, evangelical, formal, or quiet-contemplative. There are non-denominational mega-churches that attract members because they are large and ostensibly successful. Theology may or may not be an issue. Their members may be happy with the biblical miracles and a literal interpretation of scripture. Other mega-churches may be led by charismatic leaders who fulfill a need for the membership. This is not who Jesus was.

The majority of churches are small possibly having 200 members. This size is barely enough to pay a pastor and maintain a building. Smallness demands that most every member have an active role in keeping the church viable through some volunteer activity. This is good, but the disadvantage of smallness is that the financial overhead is large in comparison with the ability of its members to provide support. It cannot support major music or educational opportunities. Neither can it support major outreach programs. Merging within its own denomination is usually not possible due to geographic separation of congregations. Merging within a different denomination of similar philosophy is practical. The church of the future must be open to widening its philosophical viewpoints and becoming part of a larger grouping of churches.

The Roman Church holds fastidiously to tradition and to the dogma it developed over the last fifteen centuries. Many of its teachings and policies were developed when only the clergy were educated and its members were uneducated. Today members are educated, but the church has held that only the clergy has the authority to teach and interpret scripture. The Roman Church has not changed with society. The church has hung on to Latin as its theological language, and is locked into its hierarchical structure, which I believe it needs to shed, or at least flatten.

To hang on to celibacy within its priesthood does not make sense in our culture. Non-Catholic clergy, whether Jewish or Protestant enjoy family life, but still maintain a full devotion to their clerical profession. Paul thought that the second coming was imminent during his lifetime; therefore he concluded that marriage should be avoided. He thought everything was going to change, soon and rapidly. He preached, "don't make plans for yourself, Jesus is coming." The Catholic tradition would be richer if priests could marry and raise children. They would be no less faithful to the church if they married.

I see the Christian church as focused inward and not outward. A pet peeve of mine is to see church signboards with the title of the upcoming sermon shown on it. Multi-staff churches may even show the preacher's name. I often drive by St. Vincent DePaul's Roman Catholic Church and see on their signboard, a saying for the week. The sign may read, *"The family that prays together, stays together."* It says nothing about the homily topic for the week, nor does it give the priest's name. The church speaks to the community, not to its choir. That's what I look for in a modern church; a focus away from itself and rather to the community. I enjoy driving by that church and looking to see what gem it may offer to the public to think about each week.

Jesus sent the early Christian church out to convert the gentiles (non-Jewish and pagans) to a different set of mores. Jesus wanted people to see the world differently. He wanted them to love the Samaritans, not shun them. Today, it is not the gentiles that need to be converted, but those who profit from the poor, or those who rule by power rather than love and kindness. Jesus is still asking us to go out into the world and rescue it. It is not to add to the membership of a church, but rather to help those in power to see the world as it is, and to change injustice to justice for all.

Our foreign policies have been built around carrying a bigger stick than our enemies. Jesus advised to win your enemies by kindness not by threats. The church has this wisdom, but is not preaching to the right people. It continues to preach to itself rather than to Wall Street and to Washington.

When I visit some churches I look at their hymnals to see what their congregations are singing. Some are stuck in the early twentieth century hymnody. The language is unfamiliar and awkward with today's culture. It doesn't fit. I realize people don't like change, and churches, in general, deplore change. The seven deadly words for a church are, *"We've always done it this way before."* I have forbade any committee I have chaired to say these words in my presence. I encourage out-of-the-box thinking.

I thought that the Moral Majority some years back was headed in the right direction. I thought that it would change the perspective of Washington. I was disappointed when instead it promoted a specific agenda of getting certain laws enacted that would satisfy its particular beliefs.

The church does not exist to promote its specific theological agenda. The Moral Majority may have wanted the Lord's Prayer to be recited in public schools. A Muslim, Jew or Buddhist, may have wanted something entirely different. Our founding fathers specifically wanted to guarantee to people the freedom to practice their own religion in their own way. Neither did the fathers wish to have our government favor one religion over another.

The church should not exist to elect specific candidates, but rather to encourage people to participate and thoughtfully vote for the candidate of their choice. It may support certain legislation it deems is in the public's interest, but its job is not to promote enactment of laws that favor one theological perspective over another. Its job is to help lawmakers see society for what it is and where it is headed, and then correct injustices. The church must always seek justice, the dignity of all people, care for the disadvantaged, and integrity in all that we do.

The Need for Unification

The reason for a new church is that it can raise a voice that will be heard. Individual denominations in America will scarcely make a dent in the ethics of modern America; a unified church should have a better chance. I'll review the role of a unified church in Chapter 11, but here will confine myself to the steps that I see that should be take to make a unified church.

The Reformation is over. Now it's time for a new reformation. Let the dogma that divided us rest in the closet and be set aside for more important items. Denominations should be allowed to die a respectable death and be resurrected as a new united Christian Church. The names Protestant and Catholic should quietly fade into the past. Denominations have only moderate meaning to laypeople of today as evidenced by the growth of non-denominational churches. Those who cling to denominational ties do so either because their parents reared them in that denomination or that the style of worship is comfortable for them. Neither reason has anything to do with theology.

Reasonable Goals of Unification

It is not reasonable to expect all Protestant denominations and the Roman Catholic Church to unify. I believe the Roman church sees itself as it was born seventeen hundred years ago. It was THE church, and ever it shall be due to its mindset. What I do see feasible is that groups of like-minded denominations whose worship expressions and social philosophies are similar could comfortably join together. I can foresee conservative churches uniting. I also see that independent, and evangelical/apostolic churches might unify. Finally, I predict that liberal and mainline churches can find a home together.

The greatest needs for unification lie both at the highest and lowest levels of religion. That is, there needs to be a unified hierarchy and the smallest of the congregations need to merge together to form viable bodies. There is no reason why the church cannot have a single global mission and humanitarian aid program. There is no need to have disparate educational programs other than to represent those philosophically different groups of denominations; conservative, evangelical, and mainline. The church can survive quite nicely with a single personnel group that matches clergy and parishes. There could be no more than two or three social action groups, who probably would be formed around differing ideological bases. Even in the social arena, I believe a single group could work together to promote social justice, social care, integrity, and the dignity of all people. These goals should not be political at all, they should be Biblical.

Diversity within Unity

United Christianity does not mean that diversity must disappear. New united churches can keep their particular expressions of worship and the best of their creedal heritage. These things don't need to be changed. Those of a Baptist background should continue to immerse, and those who sprinkle should continue to sprinkle. These traditions are not significant enough to prevent unity in the face of a society that has many more problems.

What I did see when I drove through the Lower Ninth Ward of New Orleans in 2006 were up to three house-churches on the same intersection, each in buildings that might hold two dozen people each. They were all Baptist. It didn't make sense. These folks could have been part of a much larger Lower Ninth Ward church that could have had a voice that could be heard. Small towns may have a number of small churches of similar size that if they banded together could be more efficient, and stronger. Ministers don't have to lose their jobs if they are willing to work in co-pastorate churches.

Unification within Protestantism

The Unification Model

For those churches that are open to alliance with others, I see three logical groupings:

> The Progressive Christian Church
> The Evangelical Christian Church
> The Conservative Christian Church

These groupings come from philosophical similarities. The Conservative alliance might come from fundamentalist churches, those that take the Bible literally, and those of similar politically conservative groups.

An Evangelical alliance could come from the independent evangelical, charismatic, and apostolic churches that share a similar philosophy.

Progressive churches might be formed from mainline denominations with traditional expressions of worship, and hopefully at some point, include an American Catholic church. This does not mean the Catholic Church becomes Protestant, it remains Catholic, but is a part of the Christian Church, of which it has always been a mainstay.

Orthodox, Anglican, and many other denominations may choose to remain as they are or retain their traditional ties to mother churches in Europe. The process of unification would not occur in one massive step, but I believe, for the health of the church and the nation, it should occur in steps, and the sooner the better.

Churches don't have to lose their identity, only their affiliations change. For example, I see two alternatives for church names. The first line would be the church name, the second could be its affiliation. For example,

"Messiah Lutheran Church" can become,

"Messiah Christian Church"
"Progressive Churches of America"

The affiliation line could also read in a transition period:

" Lutheran Tradition"

I'd like not to see the denominational affiliation, but in a transition period it could be a reasonable compromise.

Quakers, Christian Scientists, Unitarians, and others, may or may not wish to affiliate, but they should be welcomed without having to give up their traditions and expressions of worship. Unitarians, for example, typically are socially liberal and quite active in civic affairs. As such, their alliance with Christian churches is important even if they differ on theological matters.

How does the church change from a competitive, self-preserving organism, to a collaborative group that seeks justice for all? How do we refocus our various belief systems into core beliefs that more of us can accept together, while still encouraging traditional expressions of worship?

Steps an Individual Should Take

Individuals must take their church membership seriously. By writing this book I forced myself to address the questions of faith that were important to me. I encourage individuals to do the same. You can follow my path or take your own. What is important is that you discover what is important to you, and what you feel is relevant in society today.

Small Steps Individual Churches can take

First, I would encourage churches to drop sermon titles from their signboards and offer words of advice to the community. Speak to justice and reach out to the community. The signboard is just one way. A banner can be another way. Websites can be used to spread the challenge for social justice. Letters to the Editor or politicians is yet another way to reach out.

Second, individual churches need to start discovering what they believe and why. Laypeople need to be given the opportunity to express their true beliefs. They should not parrot what they learned in Sunday school, but rather what they have learned as adults from Jesus' visit. Individual churches need to discuss what they see in society as its flaws and the reasons for them. It needs to talk about what the church can do to change society for the better.

Third, individual churches should have Social Justice committees or groups of similar title and function. Even a small church can raise its voice, but it must be organized to do so. Its adult education programs can educate its members on social issues. These are all things that laypeople can make happen.

Fourth, churches that live in proximity to each other should join together regularly to talk about social issues common to all. I remember in 1954 listening to the late J. Howard Pew, speaking at a Presbyterian Men's Convention in New York City saying that the future of the church is not within denominational ties, but rather within interdenominational ties within geographical areas. It is the churches in a neighborhood that have the greater common interest than within a denomination. I agreed with him then and see it more important today.

Fifth, I see much of the language of the church foreign to many people today, particularly the marginally religious. The King James language should be given back to the king. My exception might be the Lord's Prayer. Other than that, the *Thee's, Thine's and Thou's* should disappear. Liturgy needs to be in language that we commonly use. Hymns need lyrics that mean something in today's culture. Creative people in a congregation can develop lyrics to existing hymn tunes that are written to express what Christians must stand for today.

Finally, individual churches must talk within their congregations on what they hold as common core beliefs. Churches have glossed over their creeds and allowed their members to give lip service to what the Christian church is all about. The Bishops at Nicea developed a single short creed to sum up their beliefs in response to Constantine's ultimatum. It did not try to solve all the mysteries of God. The post-Nicaean church over the centuries expanded this basic belief system to incorporate other rather detailed dogma that ultimately led to the division of the Christian Church. It is time we pulled back together to focus on the core beliefs that could be the basis of a unified church.

This process starts with individuals within the local church. Churches need to launch interdenominational dialogue groups to talk about unification and what that would mean to them. It further involves the question; If our church were to merge with others, what is it about our faith that we would hold to, and what are those things that we could leave behind?

The Steps of the Community of Churches

There are things that must happen in the upper echelons of the church that first, close the gap among denominations, and secondly, make a difference in the world.

Neighborhood churches need to talk together and form joint committees to address social issues that affect their neighborhoods. These are not touchy-feely meetings, but discussions on real issues like homelessness, school dropout rates, and joblessness. Churches need to engage their local representatives in real dialogue on substantive issues, but they need to do this as a group.

Second, the concept of church union must be rekindled. This is not to destroy long held traditions or expressions of worship, but to reduce the divisions that separate us. Church hierarchy must accept the fact that most laypeople hold a set of core beliefs that do not include far out theological concepts that are somewhat speculative and held only as a means of trying to explain the mysteries of Heaven. To me, Heaven's mysteries can be left as such. To debate whether the Holy Spirit proceeds from the Father or the Son, is academic and has nothing to do with correcting social injustice. We as a people need to worry about what is going on here on earth. Heaven will take care of itself without our help. We have an unknowable God and He will reveal to us what we need to know.

What Denominational Leaders Must Do

Leaping ahead I see an American church that no longer has "Protestant" or "Catholic" identity tied to it. The protestations with the holy Roman Catholic Church are long past and over. If anything, a united church should have protests with society and the sick values it has pursued.

Denominations must rekindle the flames of church union. This must be done not to force rigid conformity on the church, but rather to focus on those tenets we hold in common while recognizing those traditions and expressions of worship we have no need to change. There are naturally occurring Conservative/Fundamentalist churches that take the scriptures literally. They should remain as a bloc, a unity unto themselves.

There are Evangelical/Charismatic churches that express worship in their own way who tend to be independent from hierarchical structures. These churches may be interested in forming a coalition of like-minded churches. They should be interested in social justice issues as well as other groups of churches.

There are the Mainline, Traditional, and Progressive churches that are interested in social reform, and who share similar theology. Finally, there will always be denominations that do not wish to affiliate with anyone else. So be it. The purpose of unification is to remove competition among churches and establish efficiencies in administration and programs, and that present a more effective voice in society.

Preceding the resurrection of a unified set of churches, there must occur the death of the prior denominations. Old memories must be let go, grieving must take place, but new visions must fill the vacuum left by the past organizations. Protestantism must die.

Small pieces of Roman Catholicism will fall off the Roman glacier and appear reborn as new icebergs in the sea of faith, one of which would be the American Catholic Church. This is the stuff dreams are made of. People die, but a new form of life awakens like the butterfly that springs from the cocoon. So an old form of religion may die, but a new, more vibrant and prophetic form of life should emerge if people have the vision to make it happen. Jesus will not let his church down. He will be there to strengthen it.

The steps that would occur at the national level might include:

1. Renegotiating core beliefs of faith
2. Conceiving of national organizations the could unify
3. A policy on property rights of local churches or synods
4. Unifying liturgical materials including an ecumenical hymnal
5. The theological giants need to propose concepts that recognize the historical Jesus, yet honor centuries-old traditions that we could continue to embrace, even if mythological or non-historic

I see the need for denominations to talk further about those tenets that we agree upon. We should not bicker about sprinkling and immersion, neither should we quibble about grape juice or real wine. We need to agree on those things in the Nicene Creed that we can agree to. So I see the need for a new Nicaean Council to be held. It may be a Chicago conference or one held in Albuquerque, but it should be interdenominational and have similar import to Nicea.

This first council session would probably be held only with seminary theologians. Seminary professors may tend to be more objective than denominational Bishops or clergy who may be biased by their denominational affiliations. If they laid out a platform for further discussion, then it could be held among Catholic and Protestant clergy who might ultimately comprise a unified church. The theologians, however, must deal with the historical Jesus and recommend how liturgy could be modified to acknowledge both fact and tradition in an appropriate way.

Unification within Catholicism

I believe the day is soon coming when there will be an American Catholic church disconnected from Rome. It will be formed because the traditions of the past will ring hollow in today's world. This is the same reason that gave birth to the Lutherans, the Anglican Church, then the Baptists, Presbyterians, Congregationalists and Methodists and the many others that followed. The church that is cloistered and not open to newness will be deemed irrelevant. There is too much work to do in our world to remain in a cloister. A church that is irrelevant will die.

Individual Catholic communities are already being formed. The parent church will not recognize them. They will at first be orphans. Over time they must unite and form an American Catholic Church, it would need to build a national leadership that could speak for it in a later union of Christian churches. Bishop Geoffrey Robinson deals with this topic in his book, *Confronting Power and Sex in the Catholic Church.* This would be a logical first step before further union. While the American Catholic Church may retain its veneration of Mary and the Saints, that by itself should not prevent it from being allied with former Protestant groups that call themselves "Christian." Both Catholics and Protestants are Christian. Therefore, I hold that they can be, and should be, allied.

The American Catholic Church will be driven more by the need to correct the culture in which it lives than to heed the dogma developed centuries ago. It should have married clergy and it may organize itself in a way compatible with other Christian denominations. I see it as an open church, not restricted by past decrees from Rome. It will be relevant to society and not a prisoner of the past. The church will essentially excommunicate itself from Rome, but it will find a brother in the many Christian churches that will hold it as a friend and apostolic neighbor.

The common bond among Christian churches is that God has reached out to us through His beloved Son Jesus, the Christ, who is our Lord and Savior. God raised Him from the dead, as He will those who acknowledge Him thus. Finally, He is present with us in our sacraments, and nothing will separate us from His love.

The strategy for unification must be to solely focus on what we have in common, and to leave alone the factors that have too long divided us. Perhaps what is most important is to protect our society.

National denominational organizations would not disappear so much as they would be incorporated within the broader organizations listed above. There could be a lengthy period of amalgamation.

The role of the various Councils of Churches in America would be of greater significance and different design. They would represent fewer denominations, but should have some leader for each of the three or more Christian Groups. Such a "pie in the sky" approach to religion may be considered impossible, but so were civil rights at one point. It must be done to save society from itself. I believe it can be done in twenty-five years or so. I hope that won't be too late. It starts at the bottom. A few doctoral dissertations could unearth some possibilities. Local churches must act it out together by working on common projects. This is where it starts. I encourage people to think about, and discuss some of these ideas.

CHAPTER 10

THE COLLAPSE OF EMPIRES

The Roman Empire [1,2,3,4]

When you read this section, I want you to put in the back of your mind any parallels you see between the Roman Empire and the American Empire. The unified Roman republic under Julius and Augustus Caesar reached its greatest extent at the beginning of the second century. The empire included all of Britain, Europe including Spain and Portugal, Greece, the Baltic States, the Mideast and all of northern Africa. The land area was huge. The Caesars had transformed the republic into a monarchy. The army was strong; their leaders valiant, and the nuclear Roman populations had great civic pride. There was great wealth in the Empire, primarily taken from plunder from conquered lands and taxes taken from the conquered peoples.

The success of the Empire also carried with it, the birth of its collapse. First, the conquered peoples in part collaborated with the conquerors and absorbed some of their culture. Others grew to hate the Romans and looked forward to the time when they could fight back. Second, the empire failed to develop an economic system that could be successful. Its economy was based on plunder and loot and taxes gained from their victims not on internal productivity and a positive trade balance. Third, because of their success, the army was stretched to the breaking point. A thin line of troops guarded the frontiers that could keep order within, but could never withstand a momentous attack by invaders.

An upper class developed under the Caesars that cherished ostentation, wealth, and power. They existed with the help of slave labor. The rich had gotten very rich very quickly and class stratification had set in. The lower class had steadily gotten poorer, so there was significant disparity in wealth within the Empire. Some decadence had set in with prosperity. While there were a number of factors that contributed to the Empire's collapse, no one of them was fatal in itself.

A lack of economic discipline and poor policies were major factors contributing to the collapse. When the empire had reached its zenith there were no more lands to conquer and that ended wealth from plunder and looting. The Empire had a trade deficit and little or no income from its own internal productivity. What wealth it had was spent maintaining its army, building monuments to its leaders, and catering to the needs of its upper class. The upper class paid no taxes. It was the poor that paid taxes. Because much of the work of the empire was performed by unpaid slave labor, there was little or no middle class with enough money to purchase things and contribute to the tax base. Therefore the wealth of the empire shriveled up and taxes had to be increased. When the poor couldn't pay taxes, they left the cities and took up subsistence farming elsewhere. Farmers who tilled marginal land and could pay their taxes left the empire for better living conditions far away. Food production sagged, prices went up and the inflationary spiral increased.

Another issue that helped divide the empire was that there was a division of languages and culture between east and west. Greek was the predominant language of the east and they had perhaps a more educated population. There were many Germanic type languages in Europe, however Latin was the language of the Italians and therefore, the church. As Christianity developed the east had different concepts than the west. These differences helped separate the two halves of the empire.

Defense was very problematic for the empire with an extremely long perimeter. The empire just ran out of viable native soldiers to protect its territories so it resorted to hiring Germanic mercenary soldiers. Mercenaries didn't have the training, discipline, or allegiance to central Rome as did the regulars. As a consequence, the resolve of the army diminished and its loyalties refocused away from Rome to its local commanders.

In England the barbarians from the north caused Emperor Hadrian to build a wall across the island to keep invaders out. On the continent, there were more frequent raids by barbarians both from the north and from the east. There were six major tribes in Germania[5]: the Visigoths, the Ostrogoths, the Vandals, the Burgundians, the Lombards, and the Franks. Of these tribes, only the Franks survived into the late Middle Ages. King Alaric I put the immediate pressure on the Empire during the period 395-410 CE. He led the Visigoths from the area that is now Czechoslovakia into Romania, Bulgaria and Greece, destroying Constantinople, Athens and Sparta. He then went through Yugoslavia into Italy and finally took Rome in 410 CE. The Emperor Honorius had recalled all of the troops out of Britain in 407 before the fall of Rome, but they were of little avail. Alaric sacked Rome and took whatever spoils he could find. The Visigoths then went on to the toe of Italy and King Athaulf took them north through Italy into Gaul, Spain, and Portugal where they continued their pillage.

On 1 January 406 the Vandals, Alans, and Suevi crossed the frozen Rhine River at Mainz into unguarded Roman territory. They went into Gaul, Spain, across the Strait of Gibraltar into northern Africa, then across Northern Africa and back into Italy and thence to Rome. They sacked Rome a second time in 455. By this time inhabitants had left Rome and lived in the countryside and the capital city of the Western Empire had moved to Ravenna. With the conquest of Africa, the Roman Empire lost its primary source of grain.

The final blow to the empire came when in 475 the Germanic barbarian Odoacer[6,7] rose up in the mercenary ranks of the Roman army *(foederati)* to become a commander. Emperor Julius Nepos appointed Orestes to be Magister Militum (Leader of the army) in which Odoacer was head of the *foederati*. Orestes made a deal with Odoacer that if the *foederati* would help him overthrow Emperor Nepos, he would give the *foederati* one-third of Italy as a reward. They agreed and they defeated Nepos in 475 driving Nepos into exile in Dalmatia.

Orestes seated his son Romulus Augustus as Emperor, however the Eastern Emperor did not recognize him as such. Orestes then reneged on his promise to the *foederati* so Odoacer and his troops rebelled, captured and executed Orestes. Odoacer did not want the title of Emperor, but did accept the unofficial title of King of Italy. He essentially gave the Western Empire to the control of Constantinople so the Christian empire was reunified, at least for a time. He was well supported by the people and reigned 17 years, in part because he kept Roman systems of government and law etc. in place. Many historians point to the end of the Roman Empire in 476 CE when Odoacer deposed Emperor Romulus Augustus.

Emperor Zeno of Constantinople grew jealous of Odoacer and convinced the Ostrogoth barbarians who lived within the Byzantine lands to overthrow Odoacer. This they did, and Theodoric, King of the Ostrogoths, had a three-year standoff with Odoacer at Ravenna. At a peace treaty signing in 493 between the two, Theodoric personally murdered Odoacer. The *foederati* consequently fell in line with Theodoric.

Scholars say that the Empire did not fall, but gradually decayed from bad economic policies, oppressive taxation, and finally, from the invasions by the barbarians. With the collapse of the empire, the church and invader groups filled the power vacuum.

The Symptoms of Potential Collapse in American Empire

What is it then, that will prevent or cause the American empire to fall like the Roman Empire? Will it not be in conformance with Jesus' words in Matthew 12:25 *"A nation divided against itself is laid waste, and no city or house divided against itself will stand?"*

America was divided over slavery and nearly came apart. Abraham Lincoln himself paraphrased the same words that Jesus said above. He among others saw that slavery should not be allowed and the issue was settled in an unfortunate civil war.

We were again divided over the Vietnam War and our irrational fear that Communism would take over America. Today we can easily become divided over political and religious issues, whether they are abortion rights, gay/lesbian rights, or health care issues. We have failed to reason together and have instead resorted to exaggerated claims, lies, and fear mongering.

Rome fell in part because its leadership became too far removed from the common people. The commoners, who were excessively taxed, felt they had a better future under the barbarians than their own emperors.

America is again becoming divided over what I believe is ideology. Taxpayers are irate over bailing out Wall Street then seeing the bailees award large bonuses to the executives with taxpayer money while there is huge unemployment. Healthcare reform has also divided the nation. While most people probably feel there should be health insurance reform, the timing occurred during high unemployment, which was a far higher priority for most Americans.

These may be two examples where there has been a disconnect between the government and the people. While the President is admirably trying to simultaneously tackle many difficult systemic problems in our society, the public is feeling the effects of more pressing issues such as unemployment.

I cited in Chapter three that the Evil One distorts our sense of priorities and we are suffering from these, much like the Romans did.

Things in society we need to fix

The Power of Wealth

Power comes with wealth, so we've made wealth an idol to achieve power. We live by the concept, "He who has the most money wins." The Evil One offered power to Jesus and He turned it down. Power is perhaps the number one idol in America. This does nothing to make America beautiful. It is sharing that counts, not accumulating. Sharing was demonstrated in the Biblical accounts of feeding the three and five thousand people that came to hear Jesus. These were metaphors for taking care of our brothers and sisters.

Economic Disparity

"Self over Society" has manifested itself in economic disparity. The disparity has gone into the area of "Injustice." America has promoted a significant wealth imbalance that appears to be out of control. This comes from valuing individual rights more than the rights of the community. Let's look at the disparity and actual figures, but first understand the terminology. Wealth measures the accumulation of assets a family has. This includes the cash value of real estate, cars, art, household goods, the cash value of insurance, investments and other liquid assets less any debt against these assets. This is known as a family's Net Worth. Financial wealth is a subset of net worth but it excludes non-readily liquid assets such as real estate, cars, art, or the like. Financial wealth essentially measures what a person could lay on the table tomorrow. Net income relates more to cash flow. It is gross income from all sources less expenses.

In 2004, one percent of Americans had 34.3 percent of the nation's wealth[9]. Five percent of Americans had almost 60 percent of the nation's wealth and twenty percent had 85 percent of the nation's wealth. This means that 80 percent of the people had only 15 percent of the country's wealth. In 1983 the bottom 80 percent had 18.7 percent of the nation's wealth. So the bottom stratum has lost ground in 21 years. The gap is widening as we intuitively know, but do little about.

The disparity increases if financial wealth (liquid assets) is measured. The top one percent had 42 percent of the liquid assets in the country in 2004 and the top twenty percent had nearly 93 percent. The bottom 80 percent therefore had only 7 percent of the liquid assets of the nation. It is no wonder that people lose their homes if there is but the slightest blip in employment or the economy in general. Eighty percent of the people can only afford to buy food, pay the rent, and own a second-hand car and purchase second-hand clothing. Illness or unemployment is a disaster to them.

Slavery is not necessarily dead in this country; it just has a different form. As Professor G. William Domhoff says, whose statistics I use from his paper *Who Rules America*, *"Ten percent of the people own the United States."*

The wealth of the top ten percent has increased since about 1976 due in part to tax cuts enacted by the Bush Administration that favored the wealthiest Americans. The "Trickle down" theory of the Reagan Administration did little to help the poorest Americans. They are worse off than when that theory was put forth.

Table 10.1 shows how income has changed between 1982 and 2000.

INCOME DISTRIBUTION 1982-2000[9]
Table 10.1

Year	Top 1 percent	Top 20 percent	Bottom 80 Percent
1982	12.8%	51.9%	48.1%
2000	20.0%	58.6%	41.4%

Table 10.1 shows that the rich have gotten richer and the poor have gotten poorer over the eighteen-year period shown.

Table 10.2 below shows real average annual income growth during the Clinton and Bush administrations covering the periods 1993-2000 for Clinton and 2002-2007 for Bush. Income includes compensation, capital gains, dividends, and business profits. During the Clinton administration the bottom 99 percent gathered 55 percent of the total income growth, but during the Bush administration this same group gathered only 35 percent of total income growth. This was mostly attributed to the tax cuts given to wealthier people during his administration. We can see that during this 14-year period the top one percent of income earners gained 4.5 times (5.9/1.3) the income that the rest of the nation earned.

REAL ANNUAL INCOME GROWTH 1993-2007
PERCENT BY GROUPS
Table 10.2[10]

Period	Ave. Income Ann. Growth	Top 1% Ann. Growth	Bottom 99% Ann. Growth	Pct. total growth by top 1%
Clinton Years 1993-2000	4.0	10.3	2.7	45
Bush Years 2002-2007	3.0	10.1	1.3	65
Full Period 1993-2007	2.2	5.9	1.3	50

In 2007 income for the top one percent grew 6.8 percent such that their income share was 23.9 percent of the nation's income distribution. The top ten percent of the top one percent, 14,988 families making at least $11.5m, saw their income grow 6.04 percent in 2007.

A few years back Congress fought against, but ultimately passed, raising the minimum wage to $7.25/hr[11] which would put a family of two just below the Federal Poverty Line. Of course the minimum wage for a waitress or waiter in 2009 was $2.13/hr[12] on the basis that tips would make up the difference. While the official U.S. Census Bureau poverty rate in 2008 was 13.2 percent[13] of the population, it is generally considered that 21 percent[14] of our people live below the poverty line for their sized family because the government's measuring basis has been found to be 170 percent[14] below what it should be. The poverty rate for blacks and Latinos is more than double the official rate[14]. Those legislators arguing against raising the minimum wage said that it would hurt small business. Their focus was on business, not on individuals.

Another way to look at economic disparity is the measure of multiples of the highly paid compared with the average worker making $35,000. After WWII baseball players earned about eight times the wage of the average worker. Today, a mediocre baseball player earns 60 times the wage of an average worker. The elite players earn between 400 - 650 times the average worker. Corporate executives earning $50 million receive over 1,400 times more an average worker. During the period 1990 to 2005 average worker salaries rose 4.3 percent adjusted for inflation. During the same period CEO compensation rose 298.2 percent. These statistics come from *Executive Excess, 2006,* the 13th Annual CEO Compensation Survey from the Institute for Policy Studies and United for a Fair Economy.

This disparity is economic injustice, because it is the average worker who pays for exorbitant salaries. With financial wealth has come power. There is a clique of CEO's, compliant Boards, and compensation consultants that work together to scratch each other's backs. Similarly, athletes and agents work together to ratchet up athlete's pay and agent commissions.

All this happens while an impotent government looks on, saddled by their own conflict of interests with lobbyists and other special interest groups that finance their elections.

Taxation

In addition to wealth, it is also good to look at both taxation and consumer debt, since both are key factors in the American economy. Taxes are necessary, but equitable taxation is also necessary. The ultra wealthy have some loopholes, but the poor do not. Statistics show however that the wealthy do pay their share of taxes. The top one percent paid 40.4 percent of the total income tax revenue in 2007. The top ten percent paid 71.2 percent of all taxes and the bottom 50 percent paid just three percent of all tax revenue. Of the top one percent of income earners, 98.2 percent paid taxes. Only about 4,500 persons in the top one percent paid no tax, perhaps because of loopholes. The disturbing point of the fact that half the taxpayers only pay three percent of the nation's taxes is that they are dangerously close to requiring support from the government. When this happens, the iceberg tips over.

In terms of tax rates, the highest quintile of taxpayers paid an average tax rate of about 26 percent of their taxable income. The middle quintile paid about 14 percent of their income, and the lowest quintile paid slightly less than 4 percent of their income. On balance it seems that America has a reasonable tax-sharing policy, but it isn't redistributing wealth enough to help the poor and middle class.

Some have proposed that the nation have a uniform tax rate for all. This would be a catastrophe because it would further exacerbate the disparity of wealth in the nation. The bottom 50 percent would gain little, or might actually pay higher taxes, while the wealthy would gain much more income. More people would be put into poverty and might not be able to pay the tax. The wealthy would get wealthier.

The wealthy should pay lower taxes only because their incomes should be lower. If income is shifted to the bottom 50 percent of the income pool, then they will pay more in taxes, will be less likely to file bankruptcy, and will have more to spend. The nation will be healthier if income is more evenly distributed and has fewer bankruptcies and foreclosures. It is with sales and excise taxes that lower wage people suffer because it takes a higher percentage of their money than income taxes.

Plastic Money

Americans seem to have a love affair with plastic credit cards. Business pushes consumption and the resultant purchase of goods and services. With this push to consume is the mentality of buy now and pay later. Americans are urged to enjoy "stuff" now, and pay later. Consumer debt rose from $2.2 trillion dollars to $2.6 trillion in the 4th quarter of 2008. With the recession and the outlay of stimulus money people have paid down their debt to $2.46 trillion rather than buy more goods they didn't need or couldn't afford.

The flip side to consumer debt is that the poor, with little cash, are increasingly using credit cards to buy gasoline, food, and other necessities. In this case, consumer debt is more a measure of poverty than prosperity. Because the use of plastic removes cash reality, some of this debt will end up never being paid. Through bankruptcies and foreclosures the poor will be forced to default on their credit. This will only deepen the whirlpool of economic misery. While credit may stave off the wolf for a time, the 12 percent to 15 percent interest rates that some cards carry will ultimately be the weight that drowns those poor who don't have the reserves to retire their debts. The wealthy pay their credit card balance each month so defaulted payments of the poor are made up with interest paid by the middle class.

While banks and lending institutions do all in their power to encourage credit, they do neither the nation nor its poor any favor. They only push the inevitable collapse out into the future a short time. Here again, the government must step in and restrain credit spending. Unfortunately, the government is the worst offender. Its solution is to print more money or mortgage itself to the Chinese.

Consumption over Compassion

We allow the homeless to starve, go without medical care, or freeze to death on our streets or under bridges. In contrast, business touts "materialism." There is more to life than filling our homes with "stuff" that brings no lasting satisfaction. A share of our production capability must go to providing for the needs of the homeless, and the least members of our society. Frankly, in America, there should be no homeless. We need to relate to these people.

Competition over Collaboration

Our government has created laws that favor deregulation and competition. Deregulation favors business and its profits often at the expense of the environment and employees of deregulated firms. We argue that competition will benefit the consumer. In a sense this is right, but in a sense it hasn't worked well. Many deregulated airlines have gone bankrupt and out of business. Many jobs have been lost as a result. Some airlines now pay their pilots at a level where they need food stamps to eke out a living. Industry has outsourced jobs and is squeezing the last ounces of wages and productivity out of the remaining workers.

Did you ever think of getting bids from heart surgeons and selecting the low bidder to perform your open-heart surgery? There are certain occupations where you would not want to have the least paid provider perform your services. Flying airplanes and performing surgery are two of them. Governmental regulation wasn't necessarily bad. Airlines were stable and there was a reasonable level of competition within certain heavily traveled routes. The seats were comfortable, the luggage went free, and there was a choice of good meals on dinner flights. Even with competition, the big try to swallow the small in order to eliminate competition and raise profits. Raising profits at the expense of lower comfort and safety is not in the common good.

The network television industry is quite competitive. If one network produces a doctor program, the other two are quick to copy. If one produces a lawyer program, the other two will also follow. There is little that is educational on network programming. I see that programming could improve in quality if networks collaborated to make it happen.

In politics I see little evidence of collaboration, at least between parties. The mentality is win at all costs or at least defeat the other party. We need a government that will collaborate and reason together.

Icons over Servants

Michael Jackson was an icon in the entertainment industry. As the "King of Pop" he brought enjoyment and rapture to many. Young girls went wild over his gyrations on stage. He had extraordinary performing talent. He made millions for himself and thousands for those in his entourage. This young man may have had a miserable physical existence, but many worshiped him. To attend his memorial service one had to have one of 17,500 tickets randomly distributed to the public. Unfortunately, Michael's idol seemed to be himself.

Consider Rosa Parks[15] who was arrested December 1, 1955 for refusing to give up her seat on a bus to a white man in Montgomery, Alabama. She was a seamstress, never an icon, but she did something marvelous for society. She stood up (by not relinquishing her seat) for the rights and dignity of all African Americans everywhere.

She was seated in the "colored" section of a bus in Montgomery when some white passengers got on. It was the practice of bus drivers to move the sign "colored passengers" toward the back of the bus when there were no seats available for white riders. Blacks were obligated by city ordinance to relinquish their seats to white passengers. Driver James Blake moved the sign and ordered four blacks, including Parks to move to the back of the bus. Three did, but Rosa decided enough was enough and she refused to move. Blake summoned police and Rosa was arrested. Rosa spent one night in jail and was found guilty at her trial on December 5th and fined $10 plus $4 court costs.

Rosa triggered a bus boycott the day of her trial, which ultimately lasted 381 days before the segregation policy was lifted. Parks lost her job in a department store as a result of her action and later she and her husband became unemployable in Montgomery. They moved to Virginia in 1957 to find work, and to Detroit in 1965 when she became secretary to a Michigan congressman. Her action was perhaps the key event that catapulted the young and relatively unknown pastor of the Dexter Avenue Baptist Church, the Rev. Dr. Martin Luther King Jr., into the role as the leader of the Civil Rights Movement.

King was to write in his 1958 book *Stride Toward Freedom,* *"No one can understand the action of Mrs. Parks unless he realizes that eventually the cup of endurance runs over, and the human personality cries out, 'I can take it no longer.'"*

Mrs. Parks was awarded the Presidential Medal of Freedom by President Clinton in 1996, and in 1999 the Congressional Gold Medal, among many awards by other groups late in her life. She died in 2005 and she became the first woman to lie in state in the U.S. Capital Rotunda. Over 50,000 people viewed her flag-draped casket in the Capital.

A humble seamstress does something for society, pays a price for her courage, but a popular icon lives only for himself. This is a lack of national perspective, but it also shows what one dedicated individual can do for her country with God's backing.

I listed above just some of the priorities I believe are misplaced in American society. Rome had similar misplaced priorities. For America to avoid collapse, it must change. Change won't come from inside business or the government. Neither will it come from the top of the power ladder. It will come from below. The church must look to its responsibility to be the national conscience, demanding change. Otherwise, we will all pay the price.

Some possible solutions

Define New Measures of Compensation

Compensation in our society is typically based on need and the potential value a person can bring to a firm or sports team. There also are some industry standards that have evolved. College graduates see specific salary offers that are have been standardized based on the need for a specific type person and the pool available to choose from.

Some solutions have been achieved that provides fairness for employers and employees. In baseball, for example, players used to serve under the Reserve Clause, wherein a player was tied to an owner for life, unless he was traded to another team. Now after a limited period, a player can become a free agent and offer his services to the highest bidder. Owners therefore have access to talented players if they can afford to pay the asking price. Owners have protected themselves in other sports by enacting salary caps on the team as a whole, so that the owner has a chance to make a profit.

In the corporate world salary caps do not exist. In this world, a CEO influences the selection of Board members. The Board members in turn select a compensation consultant who studies the market place and recommends CEO compensation to the Board. If the CEO is pleased with his compensation, the cycle can be repeated endlessly. The compensation consultant that recommends a decrease in executive pay would not likely be retained again, so there is little objectivity in this system. This system would seem to be based on what the company can afford, and to some extent on CEO performance. The CEO has a built-in incentive to keep corporate labor costs as low as possible so that the company shows good profits.

Employees have no say in their executive's pay. Stockholders may, at best, have a yes or no vote on director's compensation.

Some means of controlling national wealthy disparity could be:

- Wage control, i.e. salary caps
- Employee input to Executive compensation
- Industry guidelines for executive vs. company size & profits
- A set multiplier between lowest and highest company salary
- A "luxury tax" on compensation above a government set level
- Corporate bonuses to be paid proportionately to ALL employees

These are some examples of how excess compensation might be controlled. Obviously, taxing high salaries sends money to the government, but that does not get it to the people. It is best if money never leaves the company that earned it. The issue is that employees get their fare share and that the government penalizes sending jobs offshore.

I describe an example of setting a multiplier between the highest and lowest paid employee in a company. Doing this would put pressure to increase salaries at the lower end of the spectrum. If the lowest paid employee were paid $15,000/year (certainly poverty level) then a multiplier of 100 (as an example) would give the top paid person a salary of $1.5 million. If the lowest paid employee were paid $20,000 (a $5,000 gain) then the CEO could enjoy a $2.0 million salary (a $500,000 gain).

Strategists and smart lawyers would quickly say that a company should rid itself of all low paid employees and outsource instead. I would counter by saying that if a multiplier formula was used it should apply to both in-house employees or contracted outside and off-shore workers.

The point of this example is to find a different way to distribute income so the nation as a whole can be healthier. Taxing the wealthy at a higher rate is not the best solution. Giving people government handouts is not the way to restore dignity within society. Wage stabilization is perhaps the area to pursue.

Trade Imbalance

The Roman Empire suffered from a huge trade imbalance. When it lost its food supply from North Africa the nation was in trouble. America must not become an economic prisoner to another nation or bloc, like OPEC. Energy independence is a must to prevent our collapse, or to suffer a large blip in our economy.

A Stretched Military

The Roman army didn't have enough soldiers to protect its foreign perimeter. It hired mercenaries. Strangely, we are hiring private companies to provide security to our civilians working in the Middle East. I don't claim to be informed on such matters, but I believe American troops are deployed in too many places and in so doing, we are stretching our tax dollars too far. Our military dollars could go a long way to improve national infrastructure and social programs.

National Glue

Visionary leadership, truth and justice, integrity, and a common interest hold a nation together. Most of us take it for granted that we will have electricity tomorrow, that our food source will be there, and that we will have a roof over our heads. We count on our employment or retirement income being there for us. When even a few things are taken away life will become chaotic very quickly. Those who suffered through Hurricane Katrina and the Haiti earthquake know how fragile life is. The people in the Lower 9th Ward of New Orleans lost everything when the levees gave way. The residents of Port-au-Prince lost their homes and their sources of food, water, and medical care.

Society dangles by a thin strand. It can easily fall, either by natural disaster or by social upheaval. We can do little about natural disasters except be as prepared as we can to respond quickly. For social upheaval we must rely on law, justice, visionary leadership, and the church to provide prophetic vision and direction. We will delve into this topic in Chapter 11.

FOOTNOTES

[1.] Gibbon, Edward, *General Observations on the Fall of the Roman Empire in the West. Excerpts from the Internet Medieval Sourcebook*

[2.] Gill, N.S. *Reasons for the Fall of Rome – Decay – Christianity and the Vandals,* About.com

[3.] Goldberg, Eric J., *The Fall of the Roman Empire Revisited* Corcoran Dept. of History, University of Virginia, 1995

[4.] Gibbon, Edward, *General Observations On the Fall of the Roman Empire in the West, Vol. 1/Chapter 39.htm*

[5.] www.friesian.com, *Successors of Rome: Germania, pp. 395-774*

[6.] Thompson, E.A., *Romans and Barbarians: The Decline of the Western Empire, University of Wisconsin Press, Madison, 1982,* Excerpts on Odoacer

[7.] www.nndb.com, *Odoacer*

[8.] Wikipedia, *Joseph McCarthy*

[9.] Domhoff, Professor G. William, *Who Rules America,* Paper dated September 2005, University of California, Santa Cruz

[10.] Saez, Emmanuel, *Striking it Richer: The Evolution of Top Incomes in the United States (Updated with 2007 estimates),* University of California, Dept. of Economic

FOOTNOTES (Con'd)

[11.] US Dept of Labor – Wage and Hour Div. – *Fair Labor Standards Act*

[12.] US Dept of Labor – Wage and Hour Div. – *Fair Labor Standards Act*

[13.] U.S. Census Bureau, *Income, Poverty and Health Insurance Coverage in the United States: 2008*

[14.] Wikipedia, *Poverty in the United States,* citing Census Bureau statistics 3/2008

[15.] Wikipedia, *Rosa Parks*

CHAPTER 11

THE ROLE OF A UNITED CHURCH

Jesus said, "All power in heaven and on earth is given to me. Go
therefore and make disciples of all nations, baptizing them in the
name of the Father, Son, and Holy Spirit, teaching them
to observe all that I have commanded you....."Mt. 28:18-20

The Mission of the Church in the 21st century

The American church today lives in a society that could collapse. Our legislators are living with old paradigms that haven't worked. The poor are still getting poorer. Unemployment may continue to run high draining state and federal unemployment insurance accounts. Some individual churches are trying to make a difference at local levels, but the individual churches are not united as a group with a voice that can be heard at the national level.

I haven't seen the church influence a change in societal priorities other than Civil Rights legislation. Even then, it was individual leaders within the church that made the difference. Unlike the church of the Middle Ages, I do not want a church that starts wars, holds inquisitions, or seeks power for its own aggrandizement. I want a church that speaks on behalf of Christ to society to bring order out of chaos. This is what I see as a united church's mission:

- To educate itself on social justice issues and encourage debates
  and propose policies on issues that affect the ethical and
  physical welfare of all peoples

- To educate the public on issues that could destroy the country
  - (1) Economic Injustice
  - (2) Mistaken priorities
  - (3) Integrity, honesty and truth
  - (4) Care for the homeless and socially marginalized
  - (5) To work for social justice in our society

- To influence government on issues of social justice

- To reach out to corporate America and propose changes that
  would benefit all people

- To put away religious divisiveness and become a family of
  Christians once more

To achieve these goals denominations must work together to create an
organizational structure headed by an interdenominational Executive
Council that oversees committees and commissions that serve society
more efficiently than at present, such as:

(1) Social Justice Commission
(2) Communications Commission
(3) Mission Commission
(4) A Unity Commission
(5) Education Commission
(6) Property Commission
(7) Personnel Commission
(8) Liturgical Commission
(9) Commission on Ministry

These groups would:

- Encourage the amalgamation of small neighboring
  congregations of different denominations into larger churches

- Reach out and welcome the American Catholic church, when it
  forms to be a partner in a new unified Christian Church

- Change the language of the church so it becomes relevant to
  people today

I cited the Great Commission from Matthew in the chapter heading.
The objective for a unified church is *"Teaching them to observe all
things I have commanded you."* Jesus was teaching people how to
live with each other with dignity and fairness. He was giving people
a higher moral standard by which to live. Jesus was telling the people
that there was one God who loves them and was reaching out to them
so that they could be his beloved children. He was not promoting an

exclusive or specific church. He saw a universal church. He didn't want a legalistic approach to religion, but he wanted people who would love their neighbors as themselves.

Jesus wanted to heal the sick, but less the physically sick and more the morally sick. So it should be for the unified church; reach out to those who are morally blind.

Diversity within Unity

As I wrote in Chapter Nine, I wanted to make clear that a unified church does not mean the end of diversity. Differences of worship expression should remain as well as many traditions. Catholicism can keep its particular beliefs. I would only ask that it would be acceptive of the beliefs of others and look upon their fellow clergy in other denominations, men and women alike, as colleagues in ministry.

On baptism, sprinklers should sprinkle, and dunkers should dunk. Black church members should be able to shout out, "Amen brother" during the middle of a sermon if so moved.

The unified church does not have to be a conformist church. It must be a visionary church and it must reach out to society. It must make a difference in the world and in the lives of people.

Educating itself

Before a church can educate society, it must educate itself. I see this on two levels:

- Church members must know what they believe
- Church must better understand what will collapse a society

I wrote Chapters One through Eight specifically so you could see what was involved in the belief structure of the Christian Church. I also shared what I believe and the process in reaching my conclusions. I believe the church should not gloss over these things when they accept new members.

I also went through my own study of the collapse of Rome and applied that to conditions in our country today. I believe this exercise is important for all Christians.

Educating Society

At the national level the unified church can use television spots to educate. Seminars can be given, papers can be written and distributed, and sermons can be preached. Convocations can be presented at which experts can provide insights into national pitfalls on various topics. At the local level, churches can hold joint meetings with social action groups to educate interested citizens. Websites can be used, letters to editors and politicians can be written. What is important is that separate congregations get together to do these things. Tweets, blogs, and emails provide wide distribution. Even the church signboard can send messages to passersby.

Churches must join with social actions groups and not compete with them. The broadest possible bases must be formed to correct society's ills.

National Commissions

Some national groups need no explanation. A Personnel Commission can match clergy and churches. It can arrange for a more attractive benefits package for all clergy and church professionals at perhaps, better rates. One commission that might have its work cut out for it follows.

The Unity Commission

Possibly this may be a resurrection of The Council on Church Union (COCU), however I see this group as the executive commission that makes things happen. It focuses on tenets that the participants agree with and sets aside the things that have divided the church. It points itself toward success and does not exist to fail.

The purpose of this group is not to take power, but to take responsibility. Its goals are to make the church visionary, relevant, efficient, and a voice to be heard. This Commission must take disparate denominations and make them a team. It can do this only by looking forward in time, not backward

Liturgical Commission

The Liturgical Commission may have many challenges, but all are important. Here are a few of their more significant tasks:

- Recommend and codify the basic creed for the unified church, whether the Nicene, or a modification thereof.

- Deal with the questions of the historical Jesus and recommend any modifications in liturgical materials that incorporate new knowledge.

- Recommend hymnody and other liturgical materials that speak to the church in today's society using current day language.

Commission on Ministry

Among the tasks of this group would be to set the minimum standards for ordination to a pastoral ministry. Current denominations have standards, some more taxing than others, but uniform standards should be set to facilitate clergy crossing old denominational lines.

Starting the Process

I have only thrown out the seeds of ideas for what a group of unified church bodies might look like and might do (i.e. Conservative, Evangelical, Progressive). The original church was formed by a group of over 300 bishops at the instigation of one man, Constantine. I perceive it would be slightly different today. I see the process starting at the bottom with neighboring churches working together on social projects. I see state Councils of Churches playing a significant role to promote interdenominational cooperation.

Individuals must see the problem however. Individuals must see a role for the church in preventing society from collapsing. Preachers and Priests must see the problem also. They must be willing to get society to change the paradigm "Money wins" to "Democracy wins." Rosa Parks made a difference for civil rights as an individual. It will ultimately take an individual to start the ball rolling in unification.

The church universal is the only sure voice for ethical reform in the world. It cannot allow the country it serves to be run by a government of the corporation, by the corporation, and for the corporation. Our government and our laws must be for the people. Think about it, then see what you can do to make it happen.

.

BIBLIOGRAPHY

Anderson, Bernhard W., *Understanding the Old Testament,* Prentice-Hall, Inc. 3rd Ed. 1975

Borg, Marcus J. & Crossan, John Dominic, *The First Christmas,* Harper One, 2007

Bronowski, Jacob, *The Ascent of Man,* Little Brown and Company 1973

Cary, Phillip, *The History of Christian Theology, DVD Lectures,* The Teaching Company, 2008

Crossan, John Dominic, *Jesus, a Revolutionary Biography,* Harper San Francisco, 1955

Ehrman, Bart D. *God's Problem,* Harper One, 2008

Ehrman, Bart D. *Lost Christianities, DVD Lectures* The Teaching Company, 2002

Ehrman, Bart D. *From Jesus to Constantine, DVD Lectures,* The Teaching Company, 2004

Hughes, Robert D. *History, Think for Yourself about What Shaped the Church,* The Navigators, 2008

Leith, John H. *Creeds of the Churches,* Doubleday, 1963

Lerner, Michael, *The Left Hand of God,* Harper San Francisco 2006

Levine, Amy-Jill, *Great Figures of the New Testament,* DVD Lectures, The Teaching Company, 2002

Moyers, Bill, *Genesis,* Doubleday, 1996

Robinson, Bishop Geoffrey, *Confronting Power and Sex in the Catholic Church,* John Garratt Publishing 2007

Sagan, Carl, *Cosmos,* Wings Books 1980

Spong, John Shelby, *Jesus for the Non-Religious,* Harper Collins, 2007

Walker, J. Samuel, *Three Mile Island,* Univ. of California Press, 2005

Biblical Passages have been taken from *The New Oxford Annotated Bible, Revised Standard Version*

The English translation of the Koran was published by Random House, 1993

Internet Source material is shown in the Footnotes

INDEX

INDEX (CON'D)

ABOUT THE AUTHOR

Pictured is author Norm Whitcomb and cellist wife Marcia to whom this book is dedicated. Norm is a retired structural engineer and ordained Presbyterian Elder who has been a leader in the church throughout his life. He holds engineering degrees from both Tufts and Northeastern Universities. He chaired the Montview Boulevard Presbyterian Church Lectureship Committee for ten years. In that role he has been influenced to write this book by lecturers: Bishop John Shelby Spong, Marcus Borg, Walter Brueggemann, John Dominic Crossan, Bart Ehrman, Anne Lamott, Peter Gomes, Richard Rohr, James A. Forbes Jr., and others that his committee has sponsored to lecture in Denver.

Although a Bostonian by birth, Norm and Marcia live in Denver close to eight of the ten children they raised in previous marriages. Norm has also been inspired to write this book when seeing the four to six homeless, unemployed people holding cardboard signs asking for help, he and Marcia pass by on every short trip to church. This scene should not be happening in one of the wealthiest nations on earth. These are not bad or lazy people. They have been squeezed out of their jobs and homes by economic injustice in our society. He hopes to be a voice for these people.

Norm's dear friend, the Rev. William Calhoun, also encouraged him to write, and offered his comments on the text. Wife Marcia has graciously allowed him two years to write this book and six years to research and publish *The Whitcomb Family History* previously. She has kindly been his editor and punctuator, and has given him invaluable advice on the text.